Troubled Waters

Troubled Waters

Anisah Muhammad

Illustrated by Holiday Muhammad

Troubled Waters

Printed in the United States of America

ISBN: 978-1-7373534-0-9

anisahmuhammad.com

Before you proceed:

- Trigger warning: This book contains many poems related to police brutality and Black death.
- Poems with an asterisk (*) mean the poem alludes to either domestic abuse, sexual assault/rape or depression/suicide.

Allah sometimes takes us into troubled waters not to drown us but to cleanse us.

~ Unknown

To access the audiobook, scan the QR code below:

Table of Contents

'Black' and 'Muslim' and 'Woman'

Three rivers converge into the sea
Three mirrors stand to view myself
Three books of me sit on the bookshelf
Separate, yet intertwined
Divided, but mine
'Black' first, then 'Muslim' then 'Woman'
But unlike the grammatically correct placement of adjectives in a sentence
I cannot completely untwine these identities
As if they were islands
As if each one were a separate Avatar lion turtle existing independently since the beginning of time
As if each one were a

Because to be 'Black' is to be at the bottom of race
Yet to be 'Woman' is to be at the bottom of gender
And to be 'Black' and to be 'Woman' is to be the mule of the world
To be 'Muslim' is to put on bold face and to pretend not to hear them when they call you terrorist
To be 'Muslim and to be 'Woman' is to have your hijab snatched
To have evil latch themselves onto you and attempt to break you down
Attempt to turn your smiles into eternal frowns
As if you were not a human being
Less than
To be 'Black' and to be 'Muslim is to be a weapon of mass destruction
An obstruction of everything good in the world

It is to have in one hand, a gun, the other, a bomb
As if we don't have a heart for a mother's dead son
Yet to be 'Black' and 'Muslim' and 'Woman' is to hurt
Is to grieve for the girl whose rape is justified because she wore a short skirt
The boy who simply wore the wrong color of skin
The woman in a Muslim country whose laws keep her from winning
To be 'Black' and 'Muslim' and 'Woman' is to suffer three times the pain
To be at the bottom of the food chain
Yet it is also to rise despite the cage
It is to rise out of the huts of history's shame
To bring the three-fold gifts our ancestors gave
To be the dream and the hope of the helpless and the slave
To be 'Black' and 'Muslim' and 'Woman' is to reign

1. GLACIER

The Baby in the Blanket

**After the likeness of William Carlos Williams' poem:*
"The Red Wheelbarrow"

So much
depends upon
the baby in
the blanket
sleeping on the
pink cover
peacefully
on the floor.

Born into a world where
Her dark chocolate colored skin
And her cookies without the cream hair curls
Causes her to be a sexualized target
For those who would otherwise hate her

So much
depends upon
the baby in
the blanket
sleeping on the
pink cover
peacefully
on the floor.

The family cultivates her mind from day one
A doctor, a lawyer, a writer, a thinker, a great one
She will be
A sister, daughter, mother, lover
You shall see

So much
depends upon
the baby in
the blanket
sleeping on the
pink cover
peacefully
on the floor.

All of the world's problems
Are placed on her delicate shoulders
On her back
Her family rises

And in her ear
Her dead ancestors cry
Give us freedom, justice, equality
Through your eyes we will see peace
Everlasting happiness
Eternal life
Sweet child

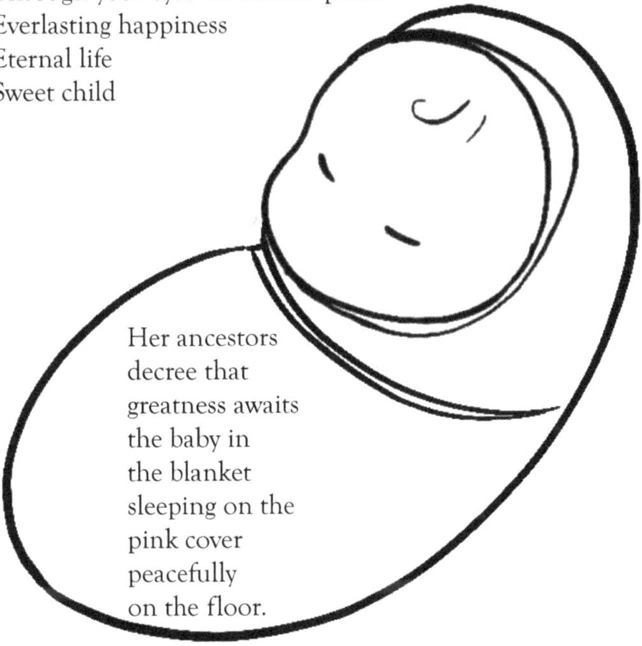

Her ancestors
decree that
greatness awaits
the baby in
the blanket
sleeping on the
pink cover
peacefully
on the floor.

Voices of my Ancestors

I'm walking down the street when I hear a cry
It's the voices of my ancestors going by
"Truth Prevails," says Sojourner Truth
Next I get a call from the telephone booth
"Hello?" I ask. "No struggle no progress"
I recognize the voice as Frederick Douglass
Harriet Tubman yells out, "You'll be free or die!"
And I'm thinking to myself, "She ain't lying"
"Character is power," says Booker T.
"Education must teach life," says W.E.B.
Noble says, "Wild animals will roam the streets,"
"Tree without roots," Garvey tells me in a beat
"Unity is more powerful than a bomb," says Elijah
Nothing better than hearing the voice of the Messiah
"KKK wears black robes," says Thurgood
Went to the courts from the lily white hoods
"A made up mind stops fear," says Rosa Parks
Oh what life do these voices spark!
Next is Fannie Lou, who's "sick and tired of being sick and tired"
James Baldwin says, "Dead embers don't start fires"
From Mandela I learn, "Education is the most powerful weapon"
"Freedom has never been free," Medgar Evers steps in
Malcolm X tells me, "The ballot or the bullet"
"Redistribute the pain," says Dr. King from the pulpit
Maya Angelou says with passion, "Still I rise"
"We ain't running no more," Kwame Ture cries
"As long as they ain't free, I ain't free," Muhammad Ali goes on
And then all the voices converge into the voice of Farrakhan

Journey in Allah's Garden

I took a deep breath of fresh knowledge
The universe expanded wide open
Now I'm moving on up, going to college
Breathing in the fresh air that knowledge provided
Wisdom and understanding gave birth to new life
Eternal journey where knowledge is rife
I took a deep breath, I sucked in all that I could
I took a deep breath, but I'm still in my childhood
Because one could never exhaust the wisdom of Allah's creation
Still, I took a deep breath and expanded my foundation
Now I'm at this point in time where I'm in motion but not moving
Because that deep breath stilled me into bettering and improving
Yes, I took a deep breath, but then

I
E
X
H
A
L
E
D

And continued through Allah's lively garden

Our Irrevocable Fate

My Ageless Ancestors reached out to me one day
"Fulfillment," they cry, they plead, they sorrowfully say
I know what they're asking, but I run, I run
They tell me my journey isn't done but has only just begun
Still, I run, I run, running to escape my destiny
Running to escape my Ageless Ancestors melancholic melody

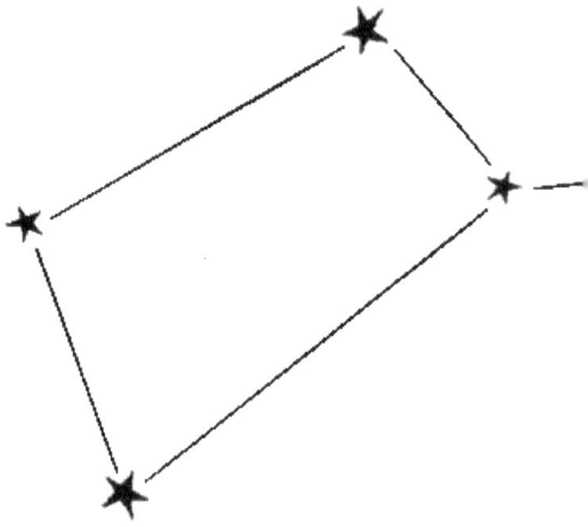

"There is no escape, you're eternally bound"
In the mouth of a cave I hide, I dare not make a sound
"You can't hide, you can't run, it's irrevocable fate"
Fast does my blood pump, increased is my heartrate
"Today is the day we wish we were alive
We didn't survive for you to deprive
Us of the freedom we sought, we strived
How dare you attempt to escape, we have not yet arrived
How dare you"

The voices catch up to me, and I don't want to construe
So I jump into a lake, drown myself, thinking finally I'm free
But I underestimated my Ageless Ancestors desire for liberty

See, a whale swallowed me whole, but why is a whale in a lake?
"See, we told you not to run, don't hate, just accept your irrevocable fate"

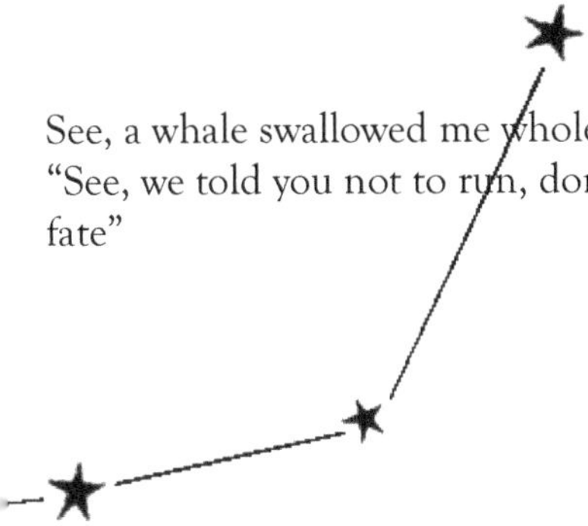

See, little by little they break me down, I'm broken
And it is only then when I can accept the wisdom that they've spoken

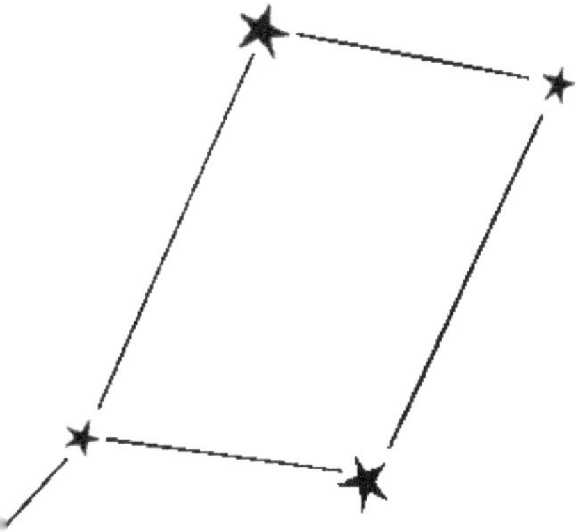

"You're tired, you're weary, just stop and listen to the old and dead
It's your time, it's your season, we already fought and bled
And don't worry, we understand, you're not a coward because you fled
For we attempted the same thing before our time when we once led
We your Ageless Ancestors are crying for our people are not yet free
It's your time to lead the cause of Freedom, Justice and Equality
Joshua Generation, stop fighting, please stand up our dear children
We need you Joshua Generation for you are the fulfillment"

And with tears in my eyes, sitting on the tongue of the whale in a lake
It's about time I accepted my irrevocable fate

The American Dream

They told me to chase the American Dream
Then they lynched my mama
Picnic by the tree
With my papa
Hanging
American Dream I can't see
How can I when
They shot my brother Tamir
My aunt Sandra
Black man turned deer
Black woman no Amanda
So how can I
How can I chase the Dream
When I'm busy looking at my
Brother bleed in the street, my
Ancestors cry
In their graves because they told me
To chase a dream I can't see
I can't see because
My people dying in Flint and
White Supremacists unleashing pent up
Rage
Like we took the country with
Obama
Even though we're still in this
Cage
No, I can't see because my uncle couldn't breathe
I can't see because my head is down and
I'm on my knees
Praying to the Black God to come save me
Because the White Jesus
Told me to chase a Dream when
The Dream was built off my nightmare, when
King's fear was
We integrated into a
Burning house

No, I can't see
This Dream you speak of, because
Dylann Roof ate
While Mike Brown was on your dinner plate
Don't tell me to chase the Dream
When you lynched my mama
Picnic by the tree
With my papa
Hanging
While I prayed on my knees
See my people die
Right in front of me
Genocide in my eyes
Too busy trying to be free
To unlock the chains
So I can be free
To liberate my people from the pain
That you put them in
We see your hypocrisy when
You tell us to chase the Dream
Though you know our hands
Are tied
And you know our people
Died
Buried in the sand
That you ask me to make footprints in
Running after a Dream
That I can't see when my uncle
Hanging from a tree
And my aunt's blood
Blowing in the breeze
You make me say "please"
For your plantation
Job
Then you call the mob when
I wear my hair in a fro, when
I go toe-to-toe with
My open enemy

So, no
I can't chase the American Dream
When I see my sister
Hanging from a tree
And my brother's blood
Blowing in the breeze
So first let me be free
But I still won't consider
Your wicked American Dream

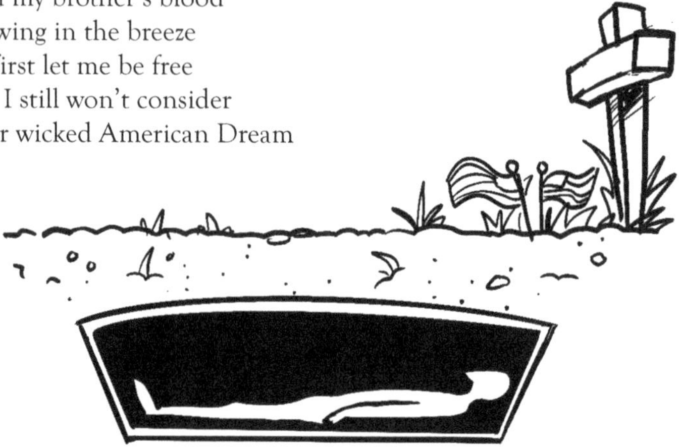

Wither in the Desert

Do not hamstring the she-camel; she gets you across the desert
But they hamstrung Obama; now the country is torn apart
He entered office with a good heart; a heart that was manipulated
He entered as a young brother; but stress made his looks degrade

Do not hamstring the she-camel; but that's what the wicked did
They hamstrung Obama; sold the country to the highest bid
Beautiful Black brother; a mercy from Almighty Allah
But they hamstrung the camel; so he's a puppet to Satan's claw

Do not hamstring the she-camel; best president the country ever had
Still they hamstrung Obama; now the people are going mad
180 turn from Obama, descend into hell under Trump
Either that or stand with Clinton, whose mouth lies are pumped

Do not hamstring the she-camel; but they did it anyway
They hamstrung Obama; now this country has to pay
Satan:Devil, Clinton:Trump, neither one of them will suffice
But they hamstrung the she-camel, so time to pay a price

He Came, He Devoured

I shall certainly come upon them
From before them and behind them
From their right and then their left
Seeking whom I may devour

He has certainly come upon the earth
From before us in the person of Trump
Lying outright and in our faces
Taking humanity to wicked places

He has certainly come unto the world
From behind us with Hillary Clinton's twirl
Smiling in our faces but secretly plotting
Lies and smiles while America is rotting

With angel steps he tiptoes light
Coming at us from our right
We think he's friend but he is foe
And so we embrace him head to toe

With heavy steps he treads the ground
Coming at us with a frown
We know he's foe but we can't fathom
The depths of this maddening phantom

With despair, I give the news
He has certainly come bringing blues
There he lied, before, behind
Right and left, on us he dined
Made a promise, didn't cower
Sought out whom has been devoured

Hell on the Horizon

America has picked her poison, hell on the horizon
Now the Electoral College everybody despising
Lucifer or Satan and looks like Satan won
I didn't elect the devil cause I didn't vote none
Can't be on the Democratic plantation when I'm trying to build a nation
Overcome this political tirade because my ancestors created creation
And the hypocrisy, forcing democracy on other countries
When your own political race contained just a bunch of lying monkeys
My first thought? I hope America is ready to go to hell
But as long as I'm with God, then in heaven I will ultimately dwell
America has picked her poison, hell on the horizon
Now the Electoral College everybody despising
But on a Clinton presidency my success did not depend
Because Asians have the lowest voter turn out and they still manage to ascend
They control the politics in their own separated communities
So why can't Blacks do the same based on our organized unity?
Because my first time being eligible to vote and two demons ran for office
And I'm sorry if my words are hurting you, but like Future I'm just being honest
My first thought? I hope America is ready to go to hell
But as long as I'm with God, then in heaven I will ultimately dwell

"Make America Great Again"

They say 'Make America Great Again' but she was never great for me
'Make America Safe Again' when my ancestors hung from trees
Make her great though my people's cry has gone unanswered
Make her safe though her evil has caused worldwide cancer
A plague to the nations of the earth is she
No, America was never great for me

They say 'Make America Great Again' but she was never great for me
'Make America Safe Again' when my ancestors hung from trees
Make her great though she's a land of unclean and hateful birds
Make her safe though she is an enemy to God's word
Disease to the nations of the earth is she
No, America was never safe for me

They say 'Make America Great Again' but she was never great to God
'Make America Safe Again' when she has spread evil abroad
Make her great though in her origins are genocide
Make her safe though hundreds of millions of people have died
Satan to the nations of the earth is she
No, America will never be great or safe for me

The Essay

"Write an essay on overcoming adversity."
Translation?
Overcoming racism

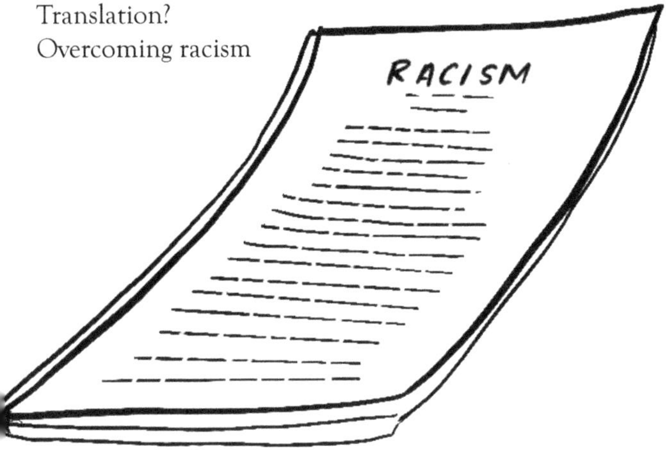

Yet the thoughts flood my mind and leave me blankly
Staring at my laptop screen
And then I blink
As if the words will write themselves
And then I blink
Contemplating on if I should be real or do the whole politically correct spiel
Like, I remember one time in kindergarten
A White girl looked at her doll and mine
She said mine was ugly because of its afro-kinky hair
And so I pulled her stringy blonde hair
And got detention for fighting
In 2nd grade there was this boy I liked
He had skin as fair and porcelain as Snow White
I told him of my crush and he scrunched his nose in disgust
And in rage I scratched his porcelain Snow White skin
And got detention
I learned my lesson at least 3rd and 4th
But in 5th Obama got elected
And my friend
Short, White with an old-lady type bob hairstyle

Started bawling her eyes out in the bathroom
And I swear her tears formed a pond that stretched for miles
Our classmates surrounded her, patted her on the back, told her it was ok
And me being me said, "At least we finally have a Black prez"
And my words went ignored because a Black prez was never supposed to see the light of day
Fast-forward to college when Trump happened
And today people scream false realities suffering from post-racial myth syndrome while I'm over here staring away at a laptop screen
And then I blink
And my fingers twitch as they itch
To type but at the same time frustrated
Because they're disconnected from the brain
Because do I really want to be another scholarship applicant filed away
Under the guise of overcoming racism *cough* I mean adversity
And agree to a system that preaches about diversity
While nothing is being done for society to overcome as a whole?
And then I blink
And my fingers type to tell sweet lies of overcoming an adversity that still plagues my life
And then I close my eyes
Because how can I overcome adversity
When in the lens of society
My Blackness is adversity personified?

The Willow's Leaves

The leaves
They fall in autumn, deprived of CO^{2} to breathe
The leaves
Where strange fruit hangs
Where dead gangbangers sway in the breeze
The willow tree
Forced to see the dead buried beneath its feet
The cement of the streets soaked with the blood of those trying to be free
The leaves listening to J. Cole singing about how all we want to do is be free
And Usher says we still in chains so Eric Garner couldn't breathe
The leaves
They fall while strange fruit still hangs
And freedom is a strange concept, so all we can do is sing
And the willow tree waits to hear the shot of the gun
Anticipation for the dead to sway in the breeze

Either that or be buried into an early grave

beneath its feet

Walking Down the Street

I walk down the street and see my brother get shot
Now my brother that killed him has to get got
Now I'm picking sides, either the red or the blue
But both are my brothers, so I don't have a clue
This Black on Black crime make me sink into hell
Revenge whispers in my ear, tolls the bell
Black lives matter but does it matter in the ghetto
When I gotta choose between the dead and the living fellow
Black lives matter when the cop shoots sixteen times
But do it matter with senseless, degenerate Black on Black crime
You got Jordans that I want so now you're dead
A five dollar bill got you in a deathbed
Taking my brother's life also took my soul
You looked at me wrong so I put you in a hole

Walking down the street and see my cuz go down
Got shot by his brother in the skin that's Brown
You my family, you my blood, so why we gotta beef?
Tired of seeing my brother's red blood soak the streets
Black lives matter so stop the killing
Stop the 6ft holes with Black bodies filling
I walk down the street and see my brother almost shot
Rather stand between the guns before my brother get got
One of the ten come to stop Black on Black hate crime
No more serving time for treating our Black selves like slime
Walking down the street arm to arm with the 10k
Til self-love is established all night and day

I Exist

I'm tired of seeing strange fruit turn into Netflix and Hulu stories
This life is too transitory
To be caught up on discriminatory comments
Like when your professor denies your existence
And dispels your experience
As if your life doesn't matter
Doesn't have meaning, as if you should be flattered
When they say racism isn't real
Because Black people steal and Black people kill so racism can't be real
Because Black on Black crime is a thing so racism can't be real
They see you as mere facts, data, stats
Bears and rats that get fat off a just system
Tell that to Botham Jean and Atatiana Jefferson
Tell that to the Black community's economic deficit
Our inability to attain the medicines
We need to heal
Racism isn't real because Black people kill
But who put the crack on paved Black streets?
Who kidnapped a people and worked them, hands and feet
Sunup to sundown and then fed them scraps instead of healthy food to eat?
Who stole a land and killed Native nations
Established plantations on Georgia's red soil soaked of blood
Tell me more about how racism isn't real
When you have sucked the lifeblood of the poor
You've reached the ceiling by standing on those on the floor
Injustice, inequality, Fergusons and Baltimores
Flints, unclean water and lead poisoning
Strange fruit documentaries, Kalief Browder, Trayvon Martin
In what setting will your heart unharden
Will the dead matter
Will my existence have meaning to a stoned being?
Yes, Black people steal
And Black people kill

But we learned from the best
We learned from the ones that progressed off of death
That stole whole nations and killed masses
Dany's Mad Queen creating ashes
Out of innocents
But the truth is, you never saw us as citizens
So it's easy to write us off as creatures that need to be brought to heel
And it's easy to see us as not real

How to Train a Racist

I wonder how you train a racist to be not racist?
Do you take them all the way back to the basics?

Do they learn racism 101, what not to do
And then change their behavior like they had a breakthrough?
Or is it more like they hide and stay hidden in the dark
And when they smell blood, they go full on shark
But then they scatter all over when the sun comes up
And issue formal apologies because of system cover-ups

Train, to teach a skill or behavior
So the racist learns to masquerade as a savior
Expert at the skill of "It's just my opinion"
Expert at "dialogue" and dictionary definitions
The racist can quote all day stats and data
To prove post-racism and that the world is better

I wonder how you train a racist to be not racist?
Do you take them all the way back to the basics?

2. MELTING

Lost in Translation

I had a Dream of the King and he said come find the real me
That got lost in translation and that desperately needs to be set free
And I told him, King, you had a brave, beautiful daring Dream
That has been wrapped up into a pretty nice bow by mainstream
King, I want you to know that you were, are, WILL always be more
Though they want to keep you as a Dream, a newly developed spore
But you're a god who evolved up until death's door

See the struggle wouldn't be no struggle without the King
And the grind wouldn't be no grind without your wedding ring
Thank you King for jumping on and marrying the freedom train
And on your last night in Memphis you said to redistribute the pain
Economic withdrawal of the corporate businessman
You said to stop buying dem red Coca-Cola cans
You said to bank Black, those those words that got lost
Your last words before you paid with your life, the ultimate cost

Somehow the Dream got lost in translation and became a nightmare
You feared you integrated your people into a burning house that haven't gotten us anywhere
Yeah somehow the Dream you dreamt, the brave, beautiful, daring Dream
Got lost in translation by the wicked mainstream
Because you're King, a god, evolved towards the solution
Black pain redistribution followed by Black liberation and revolution
They want to keep you as a Dream so we won't realize
That you're a revolutionary thinker whose last words could open eyes
Thank you, King, thank you, for working toward Black liberation
And I aim to be the you that got lost in translation

In Search of Black History

I play hide and go seek with Black History
A hidden 365-day-old mystery
I seek, I search, I attempt to find
I'm going crazy, I'm losing my mind
It's hidden so well, so deep
There's not a sign, not a peep
Maybe, I think, it's hidden behind the frozen block of Whiteness in my history book
Removed so thoroughly from the annals of history that we can't find it when we look
Maybe it's hidden behind the White man's inventions that he stole from his Black slave
Maybe it's hidden so deep that it's buried deeper than Plato's allegorical cave
I think I need a metal *cough* melanin detector to find my hidden Black queens and kings
Or maybe they're sitting right in front of me but they just don't know they're the lords of the ring
Perhaps their stolen crowns sit atop a false king's head
Perhaps our hidden history will wake us up from being The Walking Dead
I went outside one day, playing hide and go seek
Maybe if I just keep my melanin on fleek then I will hear the voice of Black History speak
I do not want to hear it from the mouth of a man masquerading as original
I do not want fictional dystopias and mythical worlds that seek to tell Black History in a storytelling visual
Unless it's Black Panther
I do not want Plato and Socrates, Homer and Shakespeare
I want my Black History that has been hidden for 400 years
I want to hold onto the thin thread of history entangling my bony fingers before it disappears
I want to know. . .what it is that mainstream fears
I went outside one day searching for a 365-day-old mystery

But then I realized my Black History is hidden inside of me
It is ingrained in our very making down to the DNA
It is our melanin on fleek slaying on the fashion runway
It is our inner Harriet Tubman and Dr. Martin Luther King
It is you, sitting in front of me, the lords of the ring

The crowns our ancestors fought and died for

Our Black History seeps out of our every pore
It circles the world and conquers 10 times in a row
It is our rhythm and flow, the vibe that makes us grow and glow and go
I went away to search for Black History yesterday
And I woke up to realize that every day Black people walk this earth is Black History day

Watering Down The Centuries of Pain

1.
You take me out of Africa
Shackle me in the holds of a ship
Then enslave me in America

2.
I'm on the auction block
You examine my physique
I'm sold because I'm good stock

3.
My children are torn away from me
Husband is raped by the slavemaster
And you force me to my knees

4.
A slave rebellion starts
And to make a fearful population
You tear his parts with a horse and cart

5.
Slavery is over, but next is Jim Crow
Deprived of basic human rights
Forced to be below

6.
Civil Rights Movement is in full swing
Crying for jobs and justice but get nothing
Still looking for freedom to ring

7.
A Black president seems to be a victory
'Post-racial America' everyone screams
But my people's death seems to be contradictory

Thus, a watered down history
Of the centuries of pain and chains
Blacks endured under the White man's reign

The Master Apologizes

**After the likeness of Kenneth Koch's poem:*
"Variations on a Theme by William Carlos Williams"

I kidnapped you from Africa to serve me with no
Pay.
I am sorry, but I had no skills to work for myself
and I saw the civilizations your people built.

We rode on the ship named Jesus
and then I deceived you.
Forgive me, for I was a Liar and a Murderer from the beginning.
I sold your mate to Johnson and your children to
Brown.
They were good stock
but I kept your daughter because she's so juicy and cold

Last evening you tried to run and I chopped your leg
Forgive me. I fear a slave rebellion, and
I wanted you here so you could know I am the master!

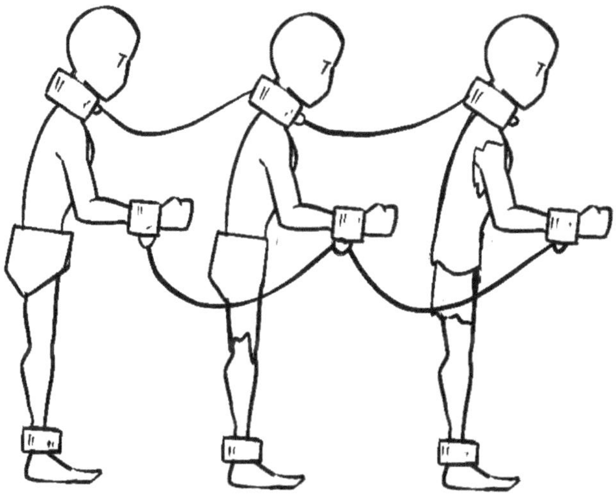

Economic Rape

Rape
- "an act of plunder, violent seizure, or abuse; despoliation; violation"
- a human atrocity forever committed upon the Black nation

My people were plundered from mother's soil, seized then transported to a strange man's plantation
To a slave man's plantation
Castrated from liberation and cremated into strange fruit
Benjamin Button syndrome as queens and kings trade their crowns and thrones for limbs shackled down and broken bones

Rape

And when I say rape I mean joining a game of Monopoly where the other players own the whole board and you're lingering in jail praying for sweet escape
And when I say jail I mean because economics were never a game you were meant to play in a strange man's land
So you tried to finesse the system, disclaim the song of the slave whip
Fight the shame your ancestors equipped but you don't have the power to rise above the status of rape victim
Sell drugs, build an empire, because that's economics right?
Rape your own people because when in strange man's land, do as the strange man does
Because victims. . .create victims
You can never rise from victim to victor as long as you suffer from slavery by another name that is sharecropping, Jim Crow, and rusty jail cells

Rape

But I don't understand how we're raped of something we never had in the first place
They come into our community and build stores of bullet-proof window casing
Muslim Arabs selling cigars and forbidden swine
Koreans doing nails and selling hair while keeping watchful eyes
Like vultures the world's immigrants flock to the economically dead
and penetrate zombie flesh, raping the rape victim twice over
And they continue to grind and rape and grind and rape and plunder and seize and despoliate and violate
Over and over the seed of the shackled slave is deposited
A human atrocity never made right with economic reparations
And the world forever wades in the river of silence

An American-Made Product

I was made in America though my origin is Africa
Slaved in America, even built the Capitol
Lost soul, no roots, I trace my history back to bondage
Lost language, though I'm bilingual, I speak English and Ebonics
America claims me as her greatest made product
Though I'm hysterical, drugged on neuroses and narcotics
She lays claim on my people like she gave fame to my people
We carved a way for ourselves out the pain she inflicted
Pain was my mother and pain married sorrow
We never thought we would ever see past tomorrow
I hear my grandmother's prayers as she cries on the cross
As my granddaddy hangs, glassy eyes on lynched moss
I hear my great, great, greats crying on the plantation
For when pain would give birth to her own Black nation
But I inherited pain's genes and sorrow's epigenetic tags
And I'm trying to make a way out, but I can't see past the tainted flag
Tainted Red, White and Blue, bloodied Star Spangled Banner
Waving the blood of my people outside of gated White Manors
I can't see past Martin Luther King's jaded corpse
I can't see past Emmett Till's face being warped
And I recognize my greatest enemy is my inner me
But I can't see a day when freedom reigns in the streets

I was made in America, American-made product
And she made profit off of me, economics and deposits
Lost soul, no roots, I trace my history back to bondage
Lost language, though I'm bilingual, I speak English and Ebonics
But then I hear pain's voice, and sorrow whispers in my heart
That through pain and sorrow comes creativity and art
The voices of all of my great, great, greats merge together
And imbue me with the powers of God's created heaven
I'm trying to make my way in, to see past sorrow's tags
To see past pain's genes, to see past the tainted flag
Tainted Red, White and Blue, bloodied Star Spangled Banner
Waving the blood of my people outside of gated White Manors
And I can see past Malcolm X's jaded corpse
I can see past Kendrick Johnson's face being warped
And I recognize my greatest enemy is my inner me
But I can see a day when freedom reigns in the streets

The Road Less Tried

You're not in it for the long-run, and you quit when it gets hard
Their whispers scar your eardrum when you should be on your guard
You make mockery of our love, but real love is long suffering
And now that I call you out, all you do is stand there stuttering
Mr. Uncle Tom sir, I thought you said we shall overcome
But now I see the false reality as you stand by your master eating crumbs
Mr. Uncle Tom sir, our love should have transcended time
But you cannot fulfill freedom's song, what's left for you is the life of mimes
No, you're not in it for the long-run, and you run away from danger
So now my enemy is your friend, and you are just a stranger
We used to walk the same path, but now we must divide
While you take the road travelled, and I take the one less tried

Uncle Tom's Battle

Like Jordin I question why love feels like a Battlefield
I say I love him but I'm still holding up a shield
He fires his weapons and I throw my stones
He tells me the Truth but I follow lying bones
I'm at war with myself because I've never been shown love
Now he comes in my life, a symbol of Peace, the white Dove
He wants me to accept my own but I reject that tone
I follow the other man to war even though he treats me wrong
I'm fighting, I'm biting, to hold on to what's not mine
Instead of building for myself and my own Black kind
Love is a battlefield, and I'm on the wrong side of this war
I'll rot in a lake of brimstone, if they say Jesus is The Door
Though I know I'm on the wrong side of the pearly white gate
I just can't help but be a shaking, bending, old Uncle Tom snake

Message to the Snakes

Three-hundred ten years of blood, sweat and tears
One-hundred forty years of post-slavery and fears
Fear that my limbs would get torn off by horses
Fear that my children would become the main dinner course
Shoot me down for sport just like you did Cecil
But Cecil getting justice, got more protection than Black people
Lion, king of the jungle more respected than Mike Brown
Lion, more respected than the fallen Black king, his fallen crown
Sphinx of Egypt, part human part lion
A sign that one day we'll rise again and march unto Zion
The New Jerusalem, great city in the sky
Half-mile by half-mile, faster than the blink of an eye
1500 Baby Planes deliver swift destruction
Bombs on Babylon at Allah's quick instruction
Spreading lies, propaganda, but the truth, you know that's Farrakhan
The truth not a truth, the discrimination, the Qur'an

Three-hundred ten years of blood, sweat and tears
Fought, bled and died but we still the prey, still the deer
Will the prey be taken from the mighty, lawful captive delivered
Prey shall be taken, Allah has need of the eagle's dinner
Wheresoever the eagles gather, there the carcass lies
Eagle is America's emblem, the country where the Black man dies
Stolen land from the Natives, Mexican man getting shut down
So-called illegal alien but White America got his stolen crown
The land, the land, all wars were fought over land
Natives got trust funds in a faithless, liar of a man
Black, Red and Brown all victims of a faithless liar
You say we starting a race war when you the one got the country on fire
For every action there's an equal and opposite reaction
Sandra Blands and Tamir Rices dying from police interaction
You expect us to remain docile? Beware when the sleeping lion wakes
Justice or Else, beware of God's wrath, this a message to the snakes

Kim K

So, I heard Kim K defending racists today
Though Kimye got children fashioned from Black clay
But see, Becky may have married Black but she ain't marry the Black struggle
And overt racism is common in the American jungle
So no surprise, no surprise, suck our Black dollars then run away
So no surprise, no surprise, that Kim K defending racists today

Dear Black Man

Dear Black man,

There's so much I need to tell you that I can't collect my thoughts
Way deep in my heart I stan for you but there's some things you ought to not
You say you're conscious, woke but then you're sexist at the same time
Sexism is not monopolized by White men, for even you have done the crime
Please don't dispel my experience, what I feel is what I feel
If I say I felt wronged by you, then just own up, admit and deal
Don't come to me with merely icing and no cake to back the sweetness up
Because what I don't need right now is a scrub, I need you to man on up
If you got a goal or mission, best believe imma help you out
But you know what I'm not? I'm not your mother so get off that couch
I don't need a son whose only purpose in life is video gaming
Cause when I see bills to be paid, good looks won't get that payment in
If you gon inhabit my vicinity then I'm gon need us to slay together
And by slay I mean pray together, be the bosses that God made us together
Imma need you to God up, be on your grind while I'm on mine
Harmonize, unify, imma need you to stay in rhyme
What it look like, I'm on the top while you laying stagnant on the ground
What it look like, you dragging me so now I'm down cause you clowned around
That ain't it Black man, if I got a mansion and you got a hut
Why minimize our blessings just cause you got an ego that leaves you stuck?

I love you Black man, and that's why I gotta constructively criticize
But you can't take it so you run to Becky, and this is why we can't enterprise
Becky got low expectations and you think she don't got attitude
Want a Black girl body but a White girl mind then wonder why my perception skewed
You can't take divinity so you run away hiding in fear
And then you got the galls to say you a real Black man, but that ain't clear
Even when you stick with me, you can't seem to take my mouth and lip
So to shut me up you turn to abuse, you decide to fight and hit
You frustrated by the system, so you bring that anger to the home
So instead of having a paradise, you make the house a hellzone
Listen to me Black man, this White world won't do you right
Accept your own and be yourself so you can really start to shine your light
Dear Black man, let's grow, unify, let's make heaven on earth, a paradise
But right now, please go somewhere, because I got a whole list and you just arrived

Dirty Laundry

A smelly shirt here
A dirty sock there
You wear your dirty laundry like you don't care

A deadbeat here
Fake woke there
I smell your dirty laundry, and I do care

You air it out on Insta, but see you think it's clean
Want your girl modest but like pictures from Playboy magazine
You say you want a queen, preach Black Girl Magic
But when Black rapists prisoned, you going "that's tragic"
You want a girl who cooks and cleans, maybe have your baby
But why would she agree when you don't treat her like a lady?
You trifling on that Playstation while she's getting her degree
Can't handle her education because you don't want her free
You make a post "my queen" but in real life she is bruised
She's supposed to be your heaven but instead she's abused
You tweet "Black man is god" and you leave her to the side
When she comments on the tweet, you let your pride rise
Your dirty laundry stinks yet you don't even know
Tell me more how you're a victim of all the isms though
You say you have been at the end of heterophobia
So we making up words, now? Well I'm fauxtepophobica
You air your dirty laundry, wear it proud on the networks
All I smell is unclean shirts, dirty socks and fake woke
Propose to me, want me forever in your life
But listed here are all the reasons I can't be your wife

Wonderland

He tells her sweet lies, whispers sweet nothings
He leads her into the rabbit hole
She finds herself imprisoned with men that see her as a toy
Red-eyed playboy rabbits
She loses herself
Attempts to find her Black Girl Magic
In a frenzy to escape a slave's fate
She accepts abuse in the form of white chocolate cake
And the fertile rabbit fertilizes the egg inside her Black folds of skin
As she shrinks inside the Wonderland
She becomes distant
Takes a journey to Neptune to escape the reality of man invading in a land she wished were her own
She fails to conjure her Black Girl Magic
She is not a magical being, she decides
She is the worker mule of the world
She is not a Black Magic Queen
Man's sweet cream attracted to her Black coffee skin
Causing her to screen herself behind a mask
She is the sexualized prey whose belly grows larger by the day
And the White rabbit abandons her
He made her dependent on creature comforts so she ends up in the clutches of the Cheshire Cat
He takes what he wills and completely disappears
And she realizes there is no magic to be found in Wonderland
No space for happiness
Still, she accepts the tea of the Mad Hatter
She tells herself she doesn't care about how every man places her on a platter
Eats her pain for their enjoyment
She sucks it up because broken creatures find comfort in other broken creatures
She knows all is vanity as they leave her one by one

She stands by her lonesome when she encounters the Queen of Hearts
The Queen tells her, "The magic lies inside
Your smile lights up a room
Your hair under water is a flower that blooms in adversity and creates a horn of cornucopia
Your eyes hold the truth of the golden sun
Your DNA holds the secrets of the universe's encyclopedia
With your nose, your lips, you conquer the beasts of the patriarchal Wonderland
You have the ability to tell your story through paper and pen and your poet's voice within
And when you create, you bring into being the cure for man's disease
Within your dark skin lies the womb of the pitch black universe
Do not retreat to Neptune nor follow White rabbits down a rabbit hole
They leave you in a false sense of wonder
The true wonder is the majesty of your Black Girl Magic
You are Original, Owner, creator of the brand new
The magic flows through your veins
Your pain prepares you for the universe's blessing"
And when she hears those words said aloud in firm voice
She screams her truth
"I am Black, I am proud
Today, I diverge from Wonderland
I am Black, I am Girl, I am
Magic"

Reclaim

I just want to let the world know that my body is mine
My body is not for you to take to gynecologist appointments to make sure my hymen is fine
It is not for you to define
When you don't make sure your son is not sticking it into another man's daughter
Creating embryos in wombed water
It is not ok, it is not fine
For you to have double standards on what is mine
On what is not yours, on what is not mans
This body, this temple, this land's physique
This divinity inside is not for you to crush with bird's beak
With so-called claims of purity while the male child runs wild in the streets
A father has no business in a daughter's affairs down there

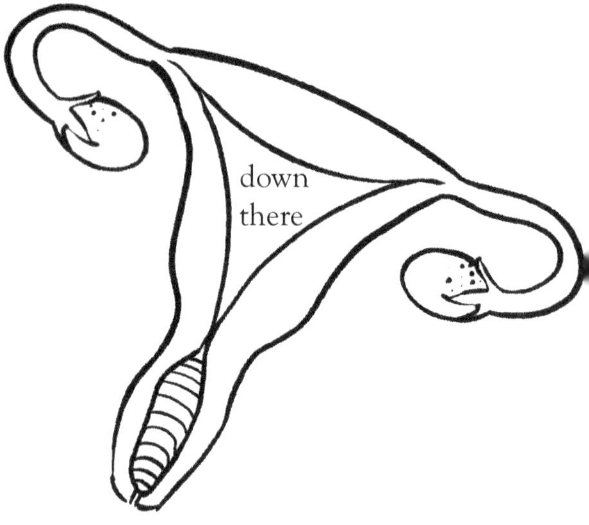

And even if her hymen did break, if her hymen did tear
That does not mean she had sex
It does not give you excuse to berate her as if she were an object, your subject to control
As if she were two-thirds of a human being instead of whole
You seem to have selective care for women
Chicks on the side and other women besides your wife
And the same ones hyping you up would shoot a woman down, metaphorically stab her with a knife
As if she's not queen, as if she's not life
Cook and clean and have my babies but no, daughter, you sit in this corner
While your brother messes over the daughter of another
So one daughter matters but the other doesn't but if you truly cared wouldn't all of the world's daughters matter?
Wouldn't you prevent men from rape, tattered clothes, life shattered
Protect all of the world's daughters from slaughter?
From wolves in sheep's clothing and teach your sons to not be the way of the wolf
To respect women, uplift her, secure her
That is pure
Pure is not you taking me to gynecologist appointments to make sure my hymen is fine
It is not you defining my body
Because today it's time for the world's daughters, it's time for me to reclaim what's mine

3. EVAPORATION

Reclaiming Black

Reclaiming Black
To push back
The Powers that be
That keep me
And my people from
Being
Completely
Free.

I Release Black Magic

Black like me
Original
But chained
Not free
Release these shackles from my mind
These chains that keep me blind
These locks that have no key
Shackles in this Black skin, we
Are Black
Original
But chained
Not free

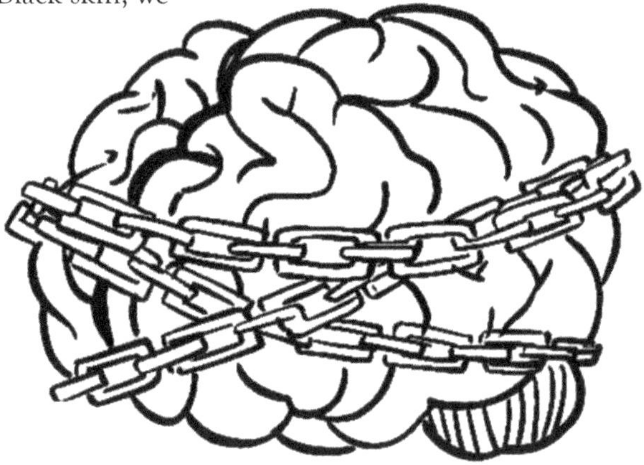

To know I could have another family
Torn apart by lands and oceans
They tell us to go back
Go back to Africa, back to the origin of Black
But how can a slave shackled
Travel in motion?
Black
R-US
Chained chattel, thus
The shop that gives little children joy
But Black is Original, not a toy
Black is not for the White man to employ
As a laughingstock as he sucks our Black Magic
Away until we are degraded
Chained classics of Black Magic
No, I am Black but comely like Solomon
I am original, old religion like Merlin
And now I command
Release these shackles from my mind
These chains that keep me blind
These locks where Black magic is key
No longer shackled in this Black skin, we
Are Black
Original
Not chained
But free

Black, Z, Pluto

They sleep on me just because I'm last
I'm used a lot less, they cast
Me aside, left to drown in the forgotten sea
All letters matter they say but apparently not Z
Because if all letters mattered then why am I treated unequally?
And I know I don't go with every word but dang all you care about is frequency
Like Pluto apparently disowned cause dang those left aside don't matter
Yeah, you say all lives matter but apparently Black life don't matter until after
We're dead in the grave, slept on like Z, disowned like Pluto
Forever subjugated, head chopped off, misery and woe
A is at the top of the totem pole, guessed in every hangman tournament
Z is the foot and A is the head so now we got superiority and judgment
But the bottom rail will rise to the top, first shall be last
I'm used a lot less, Black, Z, Pluto, forever cast
Aside, yet Pluto is a great planet rotating around the pale yellow sun
Yet Black could be a mighty people if we unify into one
Yet no sleep without Z, no zoos, zebras, or kazoos
No zoonic, zootic, zooty, zooey or zool
Probably don't even know those words because you use me like a tool
A slave just hanging at the back of the alphabet
A planet in existence that you see as a mighty threat
So you disown, don't use, wrap it up and throw it away
Cause you see power radiating from this Black human being fashioned from Black clay

Z, Pluto, Black, they sleep on us, they put us last
They use and abuse because they know deep down we're first class
Scared of our power so they won't let us flower
Keep us down in the dirt and keep the seed from April's showers
Hide our beauty, our greatness, take the credit for our talent and magic
Until we're the ones left behind, filled of faded passion
But it's time for the Z to stand, got some beef with A
It's time for the Black man to rise, shoot laser blades at what they say
Talking about we can never amount to nothing, I disagree, I disagree
How the biggest planet can be disowned, how we sleep on the letter Z
How they say all lives matter when Black ones are the ones not free
Pluto, Black, Z, the despised and rejected
Inferiority and superiority, this society is defective
Time to rise and build a new one to shine the greatness of Black, Z, Pluto
The alignment of the sun, moon, and earth and now Z-letter magic

A Bad Day at the Zoo

The zoo! The zoo! I'm going to the zoo!
The zoo! The zoo! I'm going, it's true!
Dressed, check; Down the stairs I go
Eat, shoes, car, a magnificent combo
Mama, mama, where are you? Why are you so slow?
There you are! C'mon, c'mon! Let's hurry up and go!
Driving, driving, faster, faster, I want to see a bear
Hurry, hurry, I want to see a tiger in its lair
We're here, we're here! Seatbelt gone, I'm on my way to fun
We're inside, now, under the bright summer sun
Ma look, look, look! They have monkeys and apes!
And after we see them, let's go see the snakes!
Ooo, look, he's big. Ma, you're on the phone?
Let me go closer to his zone
Oops! I fell, we're looking at each other, ma you're off your phone?
He's touching me! Ma look, we're playing in the water!
This is fun, but now I want to go play with an otter
Wait, what's that noise? What are they saying? I have no clue
Oh, wait! Watch out! Oh man. That gorilla is through

I was in blissful danger, they saved my life
A bad situation caused so much strife
But was his life really worth more than mine?
I think naught, but there's no fine line
Blaming my parents? That won't do
I just wanted a better view
Though he seemed so full of charm
He was a wild animal that could've done me harm
A bad situation has the world in a craze
But while it's sad, I'm glad I was saved

The real sad thing is if I was 12 years old
Playing with a toy gun that was sold
I would've been killed with no hesitation
No why's, no other options, and no deliberation
No support for the criminalized Black baby
No support but when you put a gorilla in the equation
You're going crazy, you're shocked, it's unbelievable
But why can't the prevention of my death be achievable?
Why can cops shoot me down and there's no cry
But now you all upset in your morals when a gorilla die
Calm down, calm down, I'm just asking...why?

These -Isms

These isms plague the earth and make me wish they were gone
Darkness seeps through their pores and blots out the light of the sun

Race-ism hitting the psyche of humans deep
Blocking salvation from the poor, Lost Sheep
False labels because Black men attracted to Becky with that good hair
While his own woman the mule of the world, forced to say a prayer
When our sons Trayvon Tamir are dead at the hand of the ism
And then we have shots giving Black boys autism
It strikes my soul when my skin is a crime so I'm
Forever a criminal forced to do time because I'm
Not aligned with the standard of beauty that is White
I'm Black, I'm Brown, I'm Red, but I'm gon' be alright

These isms plague the earth and make me wish they were gone
Darkness seeps through their pores and blots out the light of the sun
Sex-ism got me under chain lock and key
Lower pay for equal work is inequality
Hakim the wise man but I'm Hakima so why am I denied?
Force my face in the mud and rape me and take my pride
Now I'm dirty and you wonder why I'm prostituting
Even when I'm in college successfully executing
You see me as a thing to conquer, an object to possess
Compress my intelligence and subdue me with pointless sex
I'm the Mother of the Universe not a thing so make me your wife
I'm the Second Self of God so either way I'm gon' be alright

These isms plague the earth and make me wish they were gone
Darkness seeps through their pores and blots out the light of the sun

Material-ism got us heartless chasing paper and booze
Flashy cars and alcohol with some high heel shoes
Sell your daughter to continue your degenerate lifestyle
No wonder a God had to come 9,000 miles
Everyday's a party so you don't hear the knock at your door
Who is it? Death and destruction because all of a sudden you find that the galore
Is really emptiness because you're not living for a cause
Sold your soul to live the high life now you're in the shark's jaws
But sense is breaking through, it's not too late to advance to the light
Born in sin and shaped in iniquity but we gon' be alright

These isms plague the earth and make me wish they were gone
Now God is here forcing us to see the bright light of His Son

The Baby's Vision

I'm just a baby
Yes, I'm only a baby
Yet, I'm writing 'bout corruption in this
Mystery Baby-lon

I'm just a girl
Yes, I'm only a girl
Yet, I'm writing 'bout corruption in this
Wick-ed world

I'm just a child
Yes, I'm only a child
Yet, I'm writing 'bout corruption in this
Civilized wild

I'm just a baby
I'm just a girl
I'm just a child
Yet I'm writing 'bout corruption in this
Mystery Baby-lon, this - wick-ed world, this - civilized wild

I'm just a baby
But I have a vision
Cause Jesus said become like little
Children

Shelter

"Shelter," I cry out
I need sweet shelter from this bout
Of depression, from this drought
Of despair, from this current route
Along life's path
That leaves me unable to sprout
Or laugh
"Shelter," I sing in my pain
As I continue on this lane
This yellow-brick pathway
Without a place to lay
My head
And no food, water or bread
"Oh, I need shelter" I sing a sobbing song
Hoping someone can hear my longing
And with ears listening, I hear a hum
"Stay strong, it won't be long
Surely the shelter you seek is nigh
Just fly high on the wings of the sound of my voice
And when you get here, rejoice"
And then I know
That God sent a Good Samaritan my way to light the glow
To help these dead leaves sprout and grow
To pull me out of the bout of despair and go
And survive, and thrive, and live the best life
And glow, and grow, and go
"Shelter," I cry out
And shelter I have found

Will the Good Samaritan Please Stand Up

Will the Good Samaritan please stand up?
Help my people to rise above?
My people who are crying for help, asking and begging
The civilized are just walking by, passing and stepping
Is any soul brave enough to be the Good Samaritan?
To heal the dead dark people of melanin?
In a grave we've fallen and we can't get up
Crying and begging because we can't rise above
So will the Good Samaritan please stand up?
Help the mentally dead to rise above?
The civilized man walks past our distressed cry
Asking and crying but he just walks right on by
And when the Good One pulls on our melanated hand
The civilized tells him he has no right to take a stand
No right to talk about police brutality, the victims
Of White supremacy that society is endlessly
Keeping locked and tied into a system
That doesn't work for the poor, yes
Keeps the Good One from working for the Oppressed
So when Kaepernicks and Muhammad Alis
Take a stand or kneel on one knee
Then they're hated, named racists and fakes
But wait... didn't Jesus say for his namesake
Blessed is the one who men shall persecute, revile?
So will the Good Samaritan please stand up?
Help the dead dark people rise above?
Spit your poison, civilized one, and meanwhile
People are crying, asking, for a helping hand

Am I the Good Samaritan that has to lead them to the Promised Land?
Take a knee for justice, cry out for equality
Criticize the civilized man's frivolity?
I now have a duty to awaken myself to awaken my people
The Good One that will help them fly higher than an eagle
Soar into infinity, into Heaven on Earth's gate
No longer shall the melanated be in such a wretched state
Because the Good Samaritan has stood up
And has taken a vow to help the oppressed rise above

When Protest is a Crime

Freedom of speech and peaceful protesting
Peaceful protesting and freedom of speech
Colin Kaepernick and Muhammad Ali
Fighting for justice and taking a knee
Just expressing my American right to assembly
When I found myself handcuffed, locked, chained
Locked for the very thing I sought to change
Constrained, contained, and restrained
Following in the footsteps of Kaepernick and Muhammad Ali
Fighting for justice and taking a knee
Doing jail time because protest is a crime
Doing jail time because protest is a crime

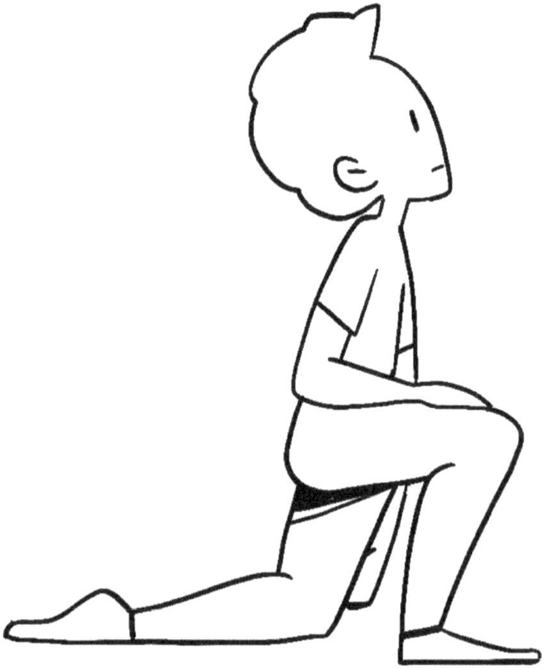

4. CONDENSATION

Rising From the Grave

Mentally stuck in a cycle of enslavement
Raging against the chains of my depravement
Get thee behind me, get thee behind
I'm blind, my mind is in decline and disaligned
Fix me, fix me, what should I do to escape this cage?
Should I pray and pray and hope that You are assuaged?
My God, my Lord, Allah where is the door?
I just want to get to Heaven, Your
Paradise I'm looking for
To escape this great war of self before
I'm completely lost to the demons of hell
Why is the air stale?
Whose funeral bells?
Blood in the air I smell
But still in this jail cell
Locked away for eternity
Stuck in a cycle of enslavement internally
Raging against the chains of my depravement

Hearing a voice that speaks volumes in my head
Sometimes you have to sleep to wake up it said
Meditation, prayer, relaxation
The demons will stay without self-exploration
Enter the deepest, darkest, dangerous dungeon of your mind
Reverse the decline to ascent, the disaligned to fine
Find your inner light and shine, and shine
On the dark dungeon demons that feed on your depravement
Why have you become satisfied in your cycle of enslavement?
See, Harriet coulda freed 1000 if they but knew
And you knew but you bathed in depression acting like there was nothing you could do
But where there's devil, there's God
Where there's Satan, there's Master Fard
You say you want to find paradise but then you're like a pig in filthy mud
You say you want to find peace but you don't let the flower bud
The light wants to get to you but you're a willing captive
God is reaching out to you but you remain static passive chattel
So, are you a slave?
Or is the Walking Dead ready to rise from the grave?

Caged Freedom

I'm running away from my caged freedom
What does freedom matter if I'm a free slave?
I'm escaping to form my own kingdom

Time to make my own self a freeman
Time to stand for myself and be brave
I'm running away from my caged freedom

No longer a captive to angelic demons
Time to satisfy this freedom I crave
I'm escaping to form my own kingdom

Thy Kingdom come, Thy will be done
Go with the flow of the freedom wave
I'm running away from my caged freedom

It's time for me to become an eagle
The will to be free is engraved
I'm escaping to form my own kingdom

I will be free, it's the time, it's the season
No longer will I be enslaved
I'm running away from my caged freedom
I'm escaping to form my own kingdom

Caged Bird Rendition

I know why the caged bird sings
As the jailer shuts off the light
'Til all that's left is shadows
Used to living in its own nest
But now as time progresses
It knows that it and its jailer sits as two separate entities
Caged identity
It is food for its enemy
I know why the caged bird sings
And why it beats its wing
In the darkness of the night
Because it feels alone
I know what it's like to need something, freedom, water, change
As the circle of life moves, I'm stuck inside this cage
I know why the caged bird utters a shrill
And why the ant builds lone anthills
But for every caged bird there is a freedom fighter
Someone that serves and moves creating change
Blocking feelings of loneliness and need
Like a dandelion in the wind
Creating love and light

An Overthinking College Student

**After the likeness of William Carlos Williams' poem: "The Red Wheelbarrow"*

So much depends upon
The sleepless
Nights
Of an
Overthinking college student

The Happy Poem Failure

Talking to my roommate like poems aren't happy
Like nothing happy in the world, sadly
But then I realized I was ungrateful
Like, the world is painful
But smile for the little things
The world is hateful
But be grateful
I'm a caged bird that sings
But at least I have a voice
I'm a slave to the balance on this thin piece of string
But at least I have a choice
Walk the sidewalk, smell the roses
The sun is shining, college closes
Just the fact we're in college
Flying on the wings of knowledge
Just the fact we woke up today
Should cause ungratefulness to seep away
Just the fact we can walk and run
Just the fact the journey was fun
May have been hard but you made some friends
May have been stressful but we're at the end
Just know why you're here, your purpose for education
Because personally, mine is here to raise the Black nation
Finals are near but troubles are here
And that's why at Mercer we major in changing the world
Talking to my roommate, can't have a poem with pearls
Happy poems are an oxymoron that you just don't do
But maybe if we stop bathing in depression then we might be able to make a few
Happiness so few of us find
We're blind, confined, and need to realign our minds

It's final exams, so what? So what?
Why don't you tell that to the man whose only dinner is a peanut?
Strutting around like a test is the worse thing ever
Tell that to the man who wasn't privileged to have an educational endeavor
See, this is why I can't make a happy poem
There's too much suffering in the world that just has to be spoken
Because if the poet doesn't speak it then will it hide in the shadows?
An elephant in the room that we plead to leave but it won't go?
And I know you came to feel good, that's why you're here
But sometimes you need to get out of your sob story so other stories can appear

I Don't Write Personal Narratives

I don't write spoken word
Or personal narratives
I write poems that are molded from my thoughts about living in an unjust world
It is easy to distance myself from the subject
To step into the shoes of a fictional character that only exists in my mind
When I hear the words "personal narrative" I am blinded by what my people have suffered as a whole
Like Elsa, I taught myself to conceal, don't feel
I don't know how to bridge the gap between this poem and you and you and this poem
During this singular moment I am speaking
I am Mr. Krabs in that one SpongeBob episode when he thought he was a robot
I am seeking to connect with you on an emotional level but I'm an unemotional being formed from mechanic bits and parts
I rock back and forth to disguise my true self in front of company
They tell me to be like Toph, to embrace the inner robot inside
I am the tin man without a heart, the cowardly lion whose friend pushes me out into the open and there is no place to hide
I distance myself from the subject and the subject from the listener
I use first-person point of view to refer to a fictional character
The character gives life to a robotic being
I don't write spoken word or personal narratives
I just write to let my thoughts of an unjust world live

The Wrong World

I think I might be in the wrong world
It feels like there is an alternate universe waiting for me to be whirled back into one soul
To be whole
And in this other world I work with the beast because the human world is at peace
I live on a farm and work with the horses and the cows
Tilling the land as my husband ploughs
And somehow this other world is truer than my existence now
Because in this current world I dislike humans but they seem to need me more than the beast because their world is not at peace
Freedom is absent in the streets so I am forced to free the voice
And in some ways it is out of duty and skill and love rather than choice
Because if it were up to me I would roam free on empty dirt roads
I would poke toads and sleep under the bird's abode like a Black Snow White
But instead I am burdened with the plights of the oppressed
Injustice, inequality, and so I use the ink and the press
I write because this world I find myself living in is unjust
For it is a world where to be woman is to be raped
To be Muslim is to be staked
To be Black is to be cursed
To be Mexican is to be deported by hearse
To be gay means to not deserve respect
To be poor means you're an insect
To be disabled means there's something wrong
To be different means you don't belong
To be me means to be held down by a world such as this one
Where the sun shines freely on all but freedom is not replicated
And so this other world is calling me, but I tell it to wait, wait
One day maybe, one day maybe my soul can escape to become whole
But as of now a stronger force is calling me to stay
To make this current world a better place

Dreams and Darkness

August 28, 1963, a man had a dream
A dream that has now been rewrapped and resold to keep the people sleep from hearing the screams in the street
See, this man that had a dream woke up from a nightmare
As he led his people to a house that had black smoke in the air
This house burned under the flames of racism
And it saw its residents turn into Netflix and Hulu stories
Streets gory, hoping one day the glory would come
But fast-forward to 2020 where little Black boys can hold hands with little White boys
So now racism is just a noise that occurred in the past, a song that's done
Professors cast your experience aside as if your life doesn't matter
Doesn't have meaning, as if you should be flattered when they say racism isn't real
Because Dr. King dispelled that, right?
As if Dr. King four years after the dream didn't talk about darkness and night
How the guilty one is he who causes the darkness
He who creates walking, living carcasses out of human beings
But because Black people steal and Black people kill, racism can't be real
Because Black on Black crime is a thing, racism can't be real
But in King's words the policymakers created discrimination
Perpetuate slums, unemployment, created the Black ghetto's frustration
1963 King experienced racism and 2020 me experiences the smart, evolved form of racism
As racists hide behind the walls of society to hide their tendencies
The walls of their university to teach "students of color"
But want to hear an enlightening discovery?
August 28, 1963, a man had a dream
But it seems to me his dream hasn't yet become reality

The Book

I am
Sitting in a park
When I hear the call of a lark
The buzzing of the bees
The squirrels in the trees
I am
Reading a book

When I hear a click
So I
Turn and look
An officer
Is holding a thick
Black handle
Finger
On the metallic trigger
Then I'm dead
Maybe in his head
He thought the book I held in my hand
Would be used to kill a man
Simply reading a book
But I guess the White cop
Simply saw me as a crook
And so now they mop
My blood, while my wife
Drops
A tear and my children
Are told by the media
That their father is a villain
The academia
Attempts to dissect what I did wrong
Meanwhile the lark's song
Is a mourning for the death
Of my last breath
And the cop high fives his buddy cop
While tears still drop
From my family's eyes
Because my despised
Black skin
Caused me
To die

Fictional Reality

Books are my life, the pages, the strife
The reality of fiction that cuts like a knife
My fictional reality is what I escape
Because when I'm awake, I suffocate
When I'm awake, I suffocate
Books cause the pain to drop to dull aches
Worlds ending and the stakes are great
Chosen ones and the stakes are great
New love but the stakes are great
In fiction, the stakes are great
And I live to read about great earthquakes
And I live to read about zombie outbreaks
Because the reality of fiction erodes away
My fictional reality that's filled with pain
And when I'm awake, I suffocate
And when I'm awake, I suffocate
Which is why I dream about stars and fate
Sleeping and dreaming about the wolf's soulmate
Dreaming and reading about fiction's golden gate
And I would rather read about dystopian slave states
Than face the reality and the horrific weight
That my fictional reality is one filled of hate
And when I'm awake, I suffocate
In a world where my Black skin is subjugate
And now I'm awake, I suffocate

Trying to Escape Reality

I get on the computer
Go to meaningless sites
Trying to escape reality

I watch television
Change it away from the news
Trying to escape reality

I play video games
Nothing violent
Trying to escape reality

I open my book
A fantasy fiction
Trying to escape reality

I face the world
With eyes closed
Trying to escape reality

I see the pain
I just turn my back
Trying to escape reality

I'm going through the actions
But just really barely existing
Because I'm busy trying to escape reality

And I think I'm succeeding

Swaying Into Consciousness

The music plays, and I sway and sway
Dancing to sweet music all night and day
Pushing my troubles aside asea
Just let me dance and leave me be

"How can you dance?" they say and say
While your people are dead from day to day
How can you push your troubles asea?
When my Black son is hanging from a tree?
Lynched, raped and you just wanna let It be

Yes, the music plays, I sway and sway
Dancing to the music all night and day
Pushing my troubles aside away
But then one day, a light, a ray
Cause we all got shot says Game one day
And Usher says we still in chains
World problems erode away my sweet escape
And so I'm left to face the reality of today

Music was a void that let me escape away
But now I'm forced to see the boy hanging and swaying
The girl shot and laying
In her own pool of blood, and the trees, the trees
Soaked with the blood of Bloody Sunday
The sky is bleak because I no longer see
The brightness of the sweet music-filled day
My ears are open to hear the true music
Of people crying, I hear them pray and pray
For a brighter day
That will never come
If people just want to sway and sway
And not hear the lyrics being cried away

Waters

There's a song in her heart that she needs the world to hear
A song too painful for one girl to bear
A silent song, a note of despair
A siren song humming softly in the air

As the girl approaches its sweet seduction
It sings a melody of death and destruction
It sucks the boat, magnetic induction
And the girl is left with deconstruction

Alone in the waters, she meets the All-Seeing
And He demystifies her of her own self-being
Now she's free from the song she was once forced to sing
And she drinks from the well in the height of spring

The waters cleanse her, clothe her, and she's made anew
She wipes her face of morning dew
The born again girl now knows her truth
And the notes of the song fade from view

Renew Reality

Every waking moment is spent philosophizing renew reality
Translating that which I see in my mind's eye into being

Renewal, to resume, to continue the acts of yesterday
Renewal, to make new again, to heal from yesteryear's pain

I am a living organism, evolving and changing
The God's prescription plan got me in-reverse ageing
Brimming with life, energy, the joy to be alive
Dumped old baggage in the trash, now I thrive

Billions of brain cells operate as one
Awake, alive, reflecting the light of the Son
His atmosphere pulls, the clash of two beings
Thus renewed again, creating renew reality

5. Precipitation

The Balance of Light and Dark

Light
Sunshine
With it is
Understanding
Knowledge of good and
Evil, a balance, yin
and yang, forces proportioned
The sun is like the human brain
Nine planets are the organ systems
Let the glow of the knowledge shine its light
On ignorance that reigns supreme in us
Let the body and the mind be one
The moon borrows light from the sun
There is no complete darkness
Light is to darkness as
Yin is to yang, good
And evil, God
and dog, sun
Moonlight
Dark

Day and Night

Day and night, yin and yang
Opposites yet they work together to produce a harmonious song
A universal language, right not wrong
The product of the earth spinning on its axis
Creating a full circle around the poles; day and night are its maxims
Yet when we zoom in to the tiny, ant-like existence of the human world
Instead of a harmonious song you see day and night that do not get along
Yin fights with yang and day fights with night
Disrupting the universal order of things
Instead of just being

Lost and Never Found

The birds are cheery, chirpy, jumping, and singing
Happy-go-lucky, dancing and spinning
Envious eyes look upon them, like how, like where
A raised eyebrow accompanied by a dead blank stare
Like how, like where can I find such playful joy
If only happiness were a toy that could be easily shared
The giddiness, the highness, the energetic lightness
The happiness, the giddiness, the sickening brightness
It blinds, it blinds and I fail to see
Why these birds in front of me are so joyously happy
While I'm down in the dumps moaning and groaning
Droning on in this poem, why my happiness has disowned me
Watch the gulls on the sea eat waves of glee
Like how, like where do I find the joyful key
To locate the carefree spirit lying dormant inside of me
Where is the key to own the energetic highness?
The giddiness, the happiness, the brightness, the lightness?
Of these birds that I look upon with envious eyes and blank stare
To be happy-go-lucky, like how, like where?
To be dancing and spinning, shining and grinning
To be cheery, chirpy, jumping, and singing

Wasted Dreams

I need a vision to take me away from reality
Edits and revisions and paint myself as something free
Perhaps a butterfly, flittering and fluttering about with joy
Or a bird, singing and stuttering and playing coy
Can I hire a builder to reshape my life into something new?
Or a mathematician to multiply into zero then add onto
It life, light and power, a seed to a flower
Nay, a wilted rose bud that even April's showers
Cannot resurrect
Why can't I have regenerative life like the phoenix
Rise up out of greatness like my ancestor's Great Sphinx
God said 'let us make light' yet I am wasting away in lightless glow
God said 'be and it is' but how can I be when I have no energy to go
With what tools can I 'be' without a vision to make 'it is'?
They say listen to what God says but how can I listen to what He says and is
When my ears only have the capacity to hear?
The voices serve as a mirror
Allowing me to hear my own reflection
Yet no human connection, none of God's perfection, just perfect rejection
Of the vision I didn't know I had
And of the dreams I wasted, so they died

Willow

I sit beneath the Willow tree
Contemplating on what it's like to be free
What it's like to be a leaf in the wind
It feels so great to pretend
That I'm a bird, unlocked and uncaged
But, I'm beneath the Willow of old age
With my life draining...draining
Maintaining the remains and barely sustaining
The life of the Willow tree
Connected to the life of me

Nisa, Are You Ok

They find me sitting beneath the willow tree
As I contemplate on what it's like to be free
They ask, "Nisa are you ok" but I don't know
I'm just so tired of growing up in a world that sucks my shine
A world where my skin is a crime

And my culture is picked,
  plucked,
    mimicked
      and
        mimed

Sometimes I wonder what it's like to be
a leaf in the wind

Or a bird unlocked and uncaged
But I'm sitting beneath this willow tree of old age

It witnessed strange fruit
hanging
Black bodies
dangling

America's seven deadly sins on full display

Her lust after strange fruit
Her gluttonous greed that sapped the strength out of me
Her slothful ways which forced me to build a country I would never be free in
Her wrath when I demand rights I that I thought the Constitution guaranteed
Her envy by keeping me at the bottom of the totem pole
Her pride in her refusal to admit wrong

They ask "Nisa are you ok" and I might not be
The willow tree's whispering touch lingers on my skin
And it stays with me as I seamlessly weave out and in
Of society's boundaries
The willows wrap themselves around my body
They strangle me yet their biting branches are invisible
It is easy to cry soft tears when I'm all alone
To let down the façade of a queen on her throne
Like Maya, I too know why the caged bird sings
It should be a crime to hang strange fruit on a southern breeze
The red soil under the foot of the willow tree
Soaked with the bloodstains of my ancestors
They ask "Nisa are you ok" but I don't have a voice to say no
My vision is blurred with the rape of my people
I need hearing aid because I never heard an apology
My balance is impaired because I never received reparations
I have anxiety from Black bodies in the street
I have diabetes from ingesting too many instances of police brutality
They ask "Nisa are you ok?"
"Are you ok?"
And all I can say

The Overtaking of Such Things

Pride is the undoing of nations,
Greed is the death of the hearts of men,
Envy is the mother of death,
And lies are told to grant false beliefs.

When we allow such things to befall us,
Our minds become the Devil's sanctuary,
Laden with false hope, false dreams,
Rendered powerless and useless,
And we become our own worst enemies.

We begin to let fear of the rising of,
Humble men,
Selfless men,
Loving men,
And truthful men,
Men who have the power of God behind them,
Overtake us.

All...
Because...
We...
Let...
Pride influence our actions,
Greed influence our hearts,
Envy influence our minds,
And lies influence our thoughts.

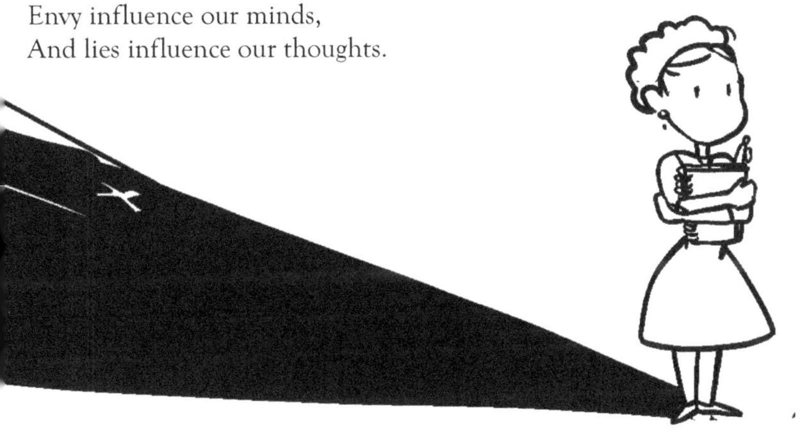

Melancholy, Sadness

Melancholy, sadness
Why do I feel
Despair, Longing
Why do I feel
Loneliness
What is this
That inhabits
My very being
My soul
Melancholy, sadness
Is it Satan himself
The Devil of self
That Self-Accusing
Spirit
Why do I feel
These feelings
That I feel
Melancholy, sadness
When will it depart

It Awakens

I'm scrolling down my social media feed when I see that Kavanaugh is free
Confirmed for the Supreme Court because sexism is the law of the land
Trump has expanded into existence the disregard for women with his right hand

It is under these circumstances that I enter into a state of disappointment
A state of dissatisfaction and resentment
That builds up to cause a cascade of electron negativity
This is my personal war against sexism and misogyny

Because like the moon was shot into space, I'm ready to blow away the world of men
Tap into anime-like powers, focus nen and write the world away from existence with my pen

The newsman asks me, "How do you feel. . ."
Well, how do you think I feel when man blames the crime on me?
When I was drunk when he took advantage and they say it's still on me?
When I wore a mini skirt when he took advantage and they say it's still on me?
I did this and I did that and he raped but it's still on me
I was flirting, promiscuous, walking alone at night
He was roaming around, searching for prey and I'm the one that caught his sight

How loud does my plea have to be for the world of men to hear?
How many have to go roughly into that good night before they know we're here?

Dear world, this is how I feel when the definition of rape gets twisted into something it's not
And the conversation shifts from the act of consent to whether I'm a thot

Yes, I'm dissatisfied, frustrated, wondering why the world is this way
Where rape apologists become the voice of reason and the heinous crime is explained away
Paint my narrative from the perspective of him instead of shining my inner truth
Social media turned sleuths investigating my story searching for a lie inside
While something precious is murdered, and something precious dies
How to get away with murder 101, just simply rape a woman
Then watch the justice system act in your favor, but trust me, God is looking
His justice will not sleep forever, there will come a day when it awakens
And I can let my

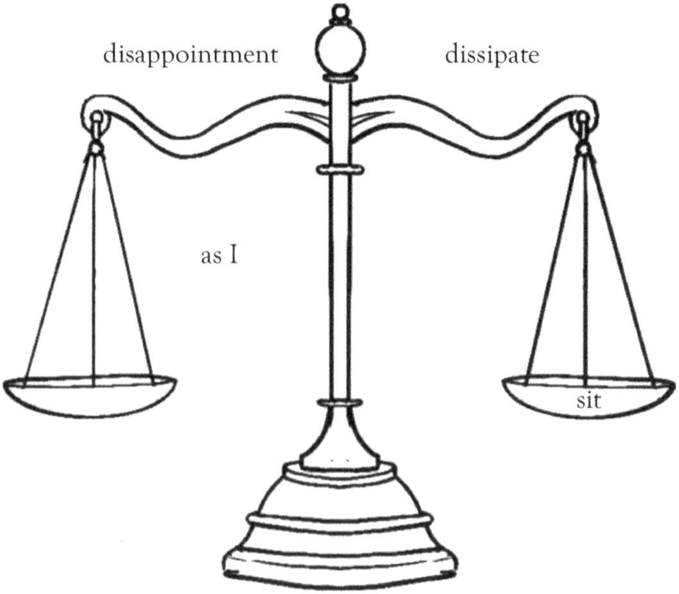

Something to Take Away the Pain

The river cleanses the mud away
The water washes the blood away
But nothing can take away the pain
But nothing
Can take away the pain
The rain drips a bloody teardrop
The trees cry leaves that mop
Away the bleeding ocean floor
As I lay sobbing against death's door
And still nothing can take away the pain
Dying is better than being slowly drained
The water washes the blood away
And now seconds feel like days
My brother is now miles away
The sun shines a sad smile
The dark of night is on the prowl
It's time to go into that good night
No energy to rage against the dying of the light
I think it's time to go away
Only death can take away the pain
Only death
Can take away the pain

A Drink of Milk

That one moment
My body felt cleansed
Clear of all pain
All of this
From
One
Drink
Of
Milk

I Found Heaven in a Cheesecake

I found heaven in a cheesecake
And in its sauce laced of strawberries
With a lake of milk by its side
And I felt very merry

I found heaven in a cheesecake
And Beatrice was the guide
The earth was made of graham crackers
And the fork, the ferry ride

I found heaven in a cheesecake
But then I broke heaven down
And now heaven is in my stomach
And the angels are out of town

Blessings

Blessings
It's not about a favorite TV show being aired
Or a new fancy product for your hair
Wearing Louis Vuitton and Gucci belts
Riding with the roof gone and no seatbelt
Got the largest house on the block so you doing well
But your inner life, family life reflect the devil's hell
Blessings
It's a part of life we don't appreciate
We block our minds, splintered thoughts from hell's gate
But it's a natural God-to-human direct deposit
Symbolic of an extra hundred in your wallet
When you avoid that accident with the car drift
You're still alive, just know that life's a gift
Peace of mind, prayers and faith with works
Being tried but having God in your network
Dial Him up on the phone and converse with Him
When you're sinking in the fire or destruction's brim
Pray, fast, then work and then the next day
You got that good job with the good pay
And you pray some more, fast some more, work some more
You got people in your life knocking at your door
Friendships in all corners and walks of life
And it started with a blessing and a little strife
Everybody wanna take the fast track
But do the fast track give you God's cashback?
A true blessing is when your soul is clear
And divinity radiates within your sphere
It's not about Louis Vuitton and Gucci belts
Riding with the roof gone and no seatbelt
It's about making the world a better place
Positive karma radiating off of human clay
Blessings

Have Faith

Close your eyes and breathe in, out
Turn left, no right to avoid that sprout
Straight a few inches, now a 25 degree
Straight a little more, watch out for that tree
Now, go back, go back, reverse that 25 degree
Turn right, no left, and you're right back at me
Now you know that whenever darkness encloses around you
Have faith in me, and my love will get you through

6. STREAM

Loud Thoughts (of an introvert), or a snapshot of thoughts when people talk to me

Come here, come closer
I have a secret I need to share
Full disclosure right now, I'm suffocating on air
As if my words are locked inside, consuming my inner being
And it's impossible to free them
Yet still, I need your ear
I need your open ear
To listen and hear what I have to say
What I'm trying to convey
Actually, if you could just open your telepathic channels, that would be great
Because these thoughts are weighing me down
And I need someone to help hold the weight
Before I drown in a sea of my own making

You see my mouth open and close like a fish
And you frown
But you don't understand my inner turmoil
Of confiding in you vs. being consumed
Because such is an introvert's plight
It's not you, it's me
No really, it's me
As I try to fight the inner demon that tells me my comfort zone is ok
You watch me sway back and forth
No, don't leave out the door
Wait
The truth is, "I –I love you."
I know it's only three little words
But understand it's hard for me to tap into my emotions
And express myself and be heard
So three little words for me to utter
Is a gigantic feat, even if I stuttered
My thoughts are loud, I don't know if you can hear
It's just, I find it hard to connect on a human level
And I second guess every worded vesicle
But... but you understand, right?
Right?

A Comma Between Love and Hate

Love
Beautiful, Precious
Caring, Touching, Adoring

Angel, Honey, Hostile, Abhorrence

Disliking, Despising, Detesting
Resentment, Repulse
Hate

Two Sides of a Coin

Why does love have to be so complicated
The dance between love and hate
Leaving me elate then frustrated, fascinated then agitated
Passions arise and we stoke the fires
Fighting and kissing trying to find balance on a thin wire
Pluck the petals, hate-love-hate-love-hate
But when I push you away, the love doesn't evaporate
Pouring salt on a fire that won't disintegrate
Stoke the fire, pour the salt, exterminate this wicked love, the hate
Passions arise and we stoke the fires
Because neither love nor hate refuse to expire
So we walk the walk, accepting fate
That this is what it must be like to be soulmates

Only One True Love

Only one true love per life
I searched and searched for the one that had the potential to forever be in my life
Went through the space-time continuum to search other dimensions
Went back millions to search hundreds of centuries
And you know what? Once I found you
I discovered that only one true love per life is true

A Sappy Love Poem

I wish I could write you a sappy love poem
Or a nice sappy song for you to hum
But I would be giving you a false view
As I've never known nor knew
What it feels like to be so in love with another
That your heart flutters at the thought
Of having one God tailor-made for you
A love so true
That his smiles make you happy
And the tears on his face leave you both in a sad embrace
A love that leaves you blindfolded, out of control
Because you don't know if it could crash and burn
In just one moment of time
You have some deep conversations and some with no reason or rhyme
You make each other younger as you swing at the park
And eat ice cream in the dark
Cuddled up watching a chick flick
He let you pick because the movie doesn't matter
Just your melodious laughter
As Sandra Bullock sings "It takes two"
"Just me and you," he sings
Tugging at your heart strings
Until you wake up and realize that it's only a false love poem
And in reality, there's no sappy singing going on

7. LAGOON

Living While Black

Walking there and here
Going back and forth
Seeking freedom's song
Chase the drinking gourd

Watch the light go out
Hide in the darkness
The sun shows its face
Reveals a carcass

Lies a dead Black man
Dared to live while Black
In the grave he lies
On his dead Black back

The living protest
Throw marches and chants
But nothing can bring
Back the dead Black king

Walking here and there
Going forth and back
Seeking freedom's song
Trying to live while Black

The Many Victims of White Supremacy

I was accused of flirting with a White woman
But because I was Black, in their eyes barely human
I was 14-years-old when I was brutally tortured
After this brutality, I was murdered
Who am I?
Emmett Till

My death was the nail in the coffin of White supremacy
I went to the store to purchase skittles and tea
George Zimmerman shot me in the chest
Protests were sparked when he didn't get arrested
Who am I?
Trayvon Martin

My friends and I were so-called perceived as threats
My killer went to eat pizza as if taking life was no sweat
Playing music too loud was my horrible crime
Now Michael Dunn is doing his time
Who am I?
Jordan Davis

I was a Black teenaged girl who got into a car crash
I knocked on the wrong door and got shot in a flash
My killer claims that for his life he was afraid
So, he took mine, but now justice is being paid
Who am I?
Renisha McBride

I was an unarmed man who got into a car crash
I was seeking help, but instead got lashed
By a Charlotte police officer I was shot 10 times
Because I am Black, my killer hasn't done time
Who am I?
Jonathan Ferrell

My organs were removed and I was stuffed with newspaper
My death is mysterious and they haven't found my invader

They claim I tripped but there's a deeper conspiracy
My organs were taken and sold is one theory
Who am I?
Kendrick Johnson

I lived in Ferguson, you know my face
Because of my death, tensions rose and tanks rolled in place
I was an unarmed teen whose crime was walking while Black
I had my hands up but the officer still attacked
Who am I?
Michael Brown

I got shot in Ohio at 12-years-old
The gun was probably fake was what the cops were told
They perceived me as an adult and did a drive-by
They say it's not White supremacy's fault but my fault I died
Who am I?
Tamir Rice

I was put into a chokehold and said I couldn't breathe
Officers subdued me as I laid underneath
I had major health problems, the life was choked out of me
My killer, Daniel Pantaleo, is still walking free
Who am I?
Eric Garner

In South Carolina a patrolman fired 8 shots
He said he feared for his life after a traffic stop
A video proved otherwise when it showed me fleeing the scene
My case is another one where an officer acts as a war machine
Who am I?
Walter Scott

I was dragged to a police van, and the officers weren't releasing
I was arrested in Baltimore and had trouble breathing
I died from an injury to my spinal cord
Officers were suspended with pay, a sign of justice being ignored
Who am I?
Freddie Gray

Rest in Peace Mike Brown

Rest in Peace Mike Brown,
May God be pleased with Mike Brown

But peace is gone because justice still hasn't come around
Crooked police killed Mike Brown, which sparked a movement on the ground
Crooked cops roam free. Human heart? No, hellhounds

Wilsons and Zimmermans masquerade while the fallen teen is left to decay
Crooked cops get first aid while families of the slain are left to pray
Beasts in human form flock together, on the mentally dead they dine and buffet
As vultures and eagles they gather with evil, and thus Black people are turned to prey

Beasts of the field that unleash blood flow
Dead in the street 4 hours made his blood soak
Through the pain we said his death wouldn't be in vain
Through the darkness a movement gave light
He was denied the simple human right
To live, and now we know his horrible plight
And though his death will never be alright
We're standing up like never before
To prevent another hashtag, no more, no more

Rest in Peace, Mike Brown
May God be pleased with Mike Brown

Another One

Anisah
I'm tired of hearing about race relations
Police brutality
You need some variation
Anisah
Why are your poems same old, same old
Same story, same victims
The same rhyme being sold
Anisah...
Anisah...Anisah...Anisah
Silence
Let me speak
Because if I don't then who?
Society will just accrue
Story after story
Narrative after narrative
Without giving the dead a voice
Because I have three brothers
They look like Trayvon
And Tamir
And Mike Brown
21, 16, and 8
I write because the dead Black boy in my poem could easily be my dead Black
brother who suffered the same fate
I write because

Oldest brother missing
Headlines
Protests
Boycotts
A hidden
Narrative
I write because he got arrested one day
And my first thought
Is this my dream
Coming into fruition?
And even though everything turned out ok
My second thought
He's obviously still alive
But I hope they didn't mistreat him
And who else will tell the stories of the ones deprived of life?
The stories of the fallen brother?

They, they, they, they
As if "they" are in another category
Us and them
We and they
As if "they" aren't people
Are other
And I recognize your humanity, Mr. Cop
But I also recognize the inhumanity of those that stop
Being human and deploy the actions of a beast
That doesn't see a fellow human AS human
But just wants to feast
On dark red blood pouring from a body
And will more good come
From writing about the cop that knows his humanity
Or the one that abandons it?

Retweet

Retweet
Because we're all social media activists summing up Black death into a post
His Twitter account's a ghost, body gone but let's retweet, retweet, retweet then roast
The racist trolls that comment and so we end up in a forever debate
But we never take the conversation outside of social media's gate
Like, retweet, retweet, repost, like, favorite, quote
Instas and SnapChat our new underground railroad steamboats
Yet we're not really involved in the struggle, we're detached
Talking about we woke when all we seem to do are hashtags
#NeverForget Trayvon Martin and Mike Brown
But what are we doing to keep the next Black target from being gunned down?
21st century Harriet Tubman so-called freeing people with a tweet
And yeah I know words are powerful but they don't stop the beasts from eating
Soaked in savagery, blood and all you can do is post a snap
On the Gram and Facebook and overlooking the real life trap
Fandoms on Tumblr but you can't tumble your way to freedom, justice
Do it yourselves on Pinterest while politicians causing do it themselves destruction

Retweet, retweet, post, favorite, like
And yeah a like can raise awareness but you leaving out the real life strike
Blocked, reported but you can't block the gun aimed at your head
And we say we're staying woke but we're all still a little dead
No progress, no change so how woke are we really, are we really?
We say we woulda stood with Harriet but she would've been real busy
Retweet this Harriet, Retweet that and pull us out of our mental cave
Free us, Harriet, free us, for we're the 1000 that know we're slaves
See, there's a place for the underground social media railroad
But sometimes we gotta go from the tweets to the streets to really attain the justice we're owed
So retweet, post, favorite, comment, like, quote, retweet
Then meet me behind the screen, #staywoke in the streets

Redistribute The Pain

Alton Sterling, say his name
But talking don't extinguish the flame
No, organize, no, boycott, redistribute the pain
All lives matter but Black lives the ones that are chained
Don't tell me all lives matter when my brother just got hanged
Handcuffed, lynched, dead, cause Black life don't matter to a devil
That's the straight up truth, Satan don't level
Kill the boy and spare the female so Philando Castile died
And they handcuffed my sister, daughter a witness to her father's cry
I could say a name, that's good, but talking don't extinguish the flame
No, organize, no, boycott, redistribute the pain
Don't tell me all lives matter when my brother just got hanged
"Should've, could've, would've's" then place the victim on blame
Crooked cops on leave while my people seeking to be free
I could say a name but the list is too long
Too lengthy, and I'm still upset over Trayvon
I could say a name, but how could I list millions
Could say a name but from 1555 to 2021 seem like we done lost billions
So if I do say a name I have to redistribute the pain

Black in America

Black girl in America, where does it get ya?
Black boy in America, where does it get ya?
Being Black in America, where does it get us?

Trayvon Martin walking home with a bag of skittles
Zimmerman comes with his lies then he gets an acquittal
Black in America with no self-defense
Being Black in America, I guess, is an offense
Zimmermans in America stalk and gun down
Seeing Blacks as criminals when they ride around town
If Trayvon was a John and Zimmerman a Tyrone
John would've got justice, in jail Tyrone would've been thrown
Has the jury reached a verdict? "Guilty! Guilty!
Throw him in jail at once! He's a savage and filthy!"
Black life gone and the killer gets awarded
What goes around comes around, justice WON'T be avoided
You see what's happening in Zimmerman's life right now
What goes around comes around, he better just avow

Black girl in America, where does it get ya?
Black boy in America, where does it get ya?
Being Black in America, where does it get us?

Kendrick Johnson, who killed him, what's the secret?
The police fight for justice, why are they being discrete?
What kind of savage mind replaces organs with newspapers
The police feed on the innocent now, they aren't saviours
The least they could do is get Kendrick Johnson justice
It's like they hold the families of victims hostage
Families becoming prisoners to so-called justice
Families with loved ones lost face injustice
The least police could do is not let Kendrick's death be in vain
Oh, I forgot, "Black life is useless," they don't feel the pain
The pain of centuries of self-hate, injustice, robbery of culture
Ohhh no, they don't feel the pain, they're like savage vultures
Taking advantage of the mentally and spiritually dead
They don't cause life they cause death and bloodshed

Black girl in America, where does it get ya?
Black boy in America, where does it get ya?
Being Black in America, where does it get us?

Renisha McBride needed help, she knocked on a door
Instead of help she got shot down on the floor
Thought nobody was home she was turning around
But, in her face she was shot and then she was down
Black girl in America went to a fellow citizen
White man in America saw her Black skin
Saw her as a threat? Shot her down in cold blood
Parents burying their daughter in the mud
That's where being Black in America gets ya
Victims of this wicked Satan Claws
Being Black in America, I guess, is a crime
Being White in America, "you're sublime"
American dream for us is a Black nightmare
We've seen the pain, felt the pain, and that's why we're scared

Black girl in America, where does it get ya?
Black boy in America, where does it get ya?
Being Black in America, where does it get us?

In Our Hearts

Emmett whistled at a White lady and got beat to death
Fast-forward to the future and Trayvon got shot
Went back 3 years and saw Oscar take his last breath
Jordan killed over music, then the traffic stop with Walter Scott
Then I turned around and saw my sister Renisha
Just like Jonathan Ferrell who wrecked his car
Women dying in custody like my sister Ralkina
'Nother Black man down, took down another star
I looked in the gym and saw my brother Kendrick Johnson
Next thing I know a cop rolled on 12-year-old Tamir Rice
Then Michael Brown killed for being Black in Ferguson
Eric Garner couldn't breathe and they sucking our life
Freddie Gray abused in Baltimore, our blood soaks the land
Raynette dead in New York, Kindra Chapman Alabama
Looked in a Texas jail and saw my sister Sandra Bland
Police lie but the truth is on the dash camera

Emmett Till, Trayvon Martin, Oscar Grant, fallen kings
Jordan Davis, Walter Scott, my brothers living
Renisha McBride, Jonathan Ferrell, live on
Ralkina Jones, infinity and beyond
Kendrick Johnson and Tamir Rice are here
Mike Brown and Eric Garner did not disappear
Freddie Gray and Raynette Turner are alive
Kindra Chapman and Sandra Bland still thrive

They're in our hearts forever, trust and believe they won't die
The fight is not over, because the oppressed still cry

8. WATERFALL

The World Goes by in a Blur

The world goes by in a blur
Leaving anyone and everyone
You better keep up

The world goes by in a blur
Not caring to stop for anyone
Not caring for a pause

The world goes by in a blur
Whether we like it or not
There's no slowing down the inevitable

The world goes by in a blur
And whoever can't keep up
Will be lost observing forever

The world goes by in a blur
And it would suck to be stuck on the sidelines
Watching, waiting, but it will already have passed

The world goes by in a blur
Either keep up the pace
Or be lost in its footsteps

The world goes by in a blur
It's your choice to live for tomorrow
Or be stuck in the past forever

Blank

The canvas is blank, waiting for something of substance
Something to make meaning of its existence just this once
Something to trust in
The artist sits
Staring blankly at blank canvas as if it can commit to painting itself
As if it could transmit what it wants to be written
And what can blank canvas and blank artist produce?

None The Wiser

Wednesday I turned 21
The Sunday before, my family treated me to dinner
The Saturday before, I broke down and cried
Yet the Sunday after, I smiled
The Wednesday I turned 21, I smiled
And no one is none the wiser

I don't cry
I bottle up my emotions
Maybe the bottle was full
There simply wasn't enough space
So the bottle cracked

I don't know why I cried
I have no reason to cry
I'm blessed
Right?

I have enough money to buy what I need
Small jobs
A family that loves me
Friends that care about me

But I still cried

I like to write
I think that's my purpose in life
I enjoy reading
Movies
But I can't find reason in my own story

I cried

And I thought about Willow Smith
She cut herself
Because her outward circumstances
Weren't reflecting the inside
The cut is tangible

I cried

It came out of nowhere
And it left like a ghost

I'm not depressed
I have severe bouts of sadness, sure
I contemplate the meaning of life
Sometimes I feel like I'm slowly wasting away
But that's not the reason
The reason is unknown
It was a brief cry
A brief yet long intense cry
And afterward
I went about my life
Like nothing happened

Like Tamia
I put a smile on my face
And if anyone asks me
Everything is ok
I'm laughing
But I'm dying inside
With a smile on my face

Wednesday I turned 21
The Sunday before, my family treated me to dinner
The Saturday before, I broke down and cried
Yet the Sunday after, I smiled
The Wednesday I turned 21, I smiled
And no one is none the wiser

Something Lost

I think I've been hit by an energy vampire
I think it's sucking my spiritual life away
I think it's the devil's angel for hire
No wonder I'm bleeding from pain today

Out of nowhere sudden bouts of sadness come
I'm not depressed but I also don't know what's wrong
All strength is sapped and I'm left numb
Day in and day out, all the day long

I question if I'm being ungrateful
Though I know I'm thankful for being alive
I still feel empty in a room full of people
When will happiness arrive?

Is it that I feel purposeless?
I have no reason to feel that way
Was I not born to be a journalist?
I don't understand why I'm seeing black and grey

It really only happens when I'm alone
Where I can unmask my suffering in quietude
The rest of the world thinks I'm a queen on her throne
When inside I'm in a tumultuous mood

Something is sucking my life's blood away
Out of nowhere random bouts of sadness come
I don't understand why I'm seeing tones of grey
How can I regain my queenly throne?

Battling Sadness

I feel intense sadness,
Deep inside of me.
I feel intense pain,
Keeping me from being free.

Something's holding me back,
But I don't know what.
Something deep inside,
Has me in a rut.

I put on a smile,
That is easy to feign.
Every new day,
I live with the pain.

My soul is unsatisfied,
Searching for purpose.
Don't know what I want,
My thoughts are a circus.

Soft tears come,
When I'm all alone.
This shouldn't be the attitude,
Of a queen on her throne.

Occasionally I realize,
I have strength and willpower.
I spring from my roots,
And sprout up like a flower.

I take in positivity,
The water that gives me life.
The sadness goes away,
Until a far off night.

Seasons

Sweat glistened off my forehead
Tank top on
Shorts on
Sandals on
But why was I still burning
My hair ignited into flames
The light flickered in my eyes
I squinted
Summer

The leaves rained on my face
Oranges, Yellows, Reds, Browns
It was a race
A race to see who could make it to the ground faster
I looked up
Up into the pouring leaves
I knew that as soon as they touched the ground
They would eventually rot and die
But did they know this
Fall

Dead
Everything is dead
Where are the singing birds
The jumping squirrels
Even the trees are dead
I walked out
The coldness stung my face
My warmest clothes on
I could still feel the bitterness of the wind
Winter

I sat under the shady tree
Listened to the noises of nature
The buzzing of the bees
The chirping of the birds
The energized squirrels chased each other
Even the tiny ant seemed enlivened
Flowers bloomed
Nature was full of life
But why wasn't I
The rain came pouring down
Washed away the tears from my eyes
Spring

Changes

Life is a revolving door with ups and downs, moons and suns
The door opens and shuts like babies born and funeral homes
Yet life's cyclical motion escapes me
I sit by a tree in the park and watch children swing, up and down, up and down
Sliding and climbing on the playground
Yet their joy does not reach me
I'm on a journey searching for life's buried treasure chest
But the path elongates and I need rest
And I tell myself I'm just in between blessings
Like every step I take forward is a past step blocked
So I can't go backward, I just have to keep walking
Until I discover what it is the universe has for me
Maybe the key buried in the sea under the sands of Atlantis
Or childlike laughter as I blissfully swing in the summer's heat
Listening to Tupac's 'Changes' and tapping along to the beat
Until life's revolving door pulls me into its game
And I'm never the same

Flawed Though I Be

I am a planet circulating around a big ball of gas
The tiny star that looks to the example of the bright light that basks
From the sun
And parades in its atmosphere as the earth is spun
Everything I am, everything I do, my sole goal in life is oneness with God
But how, you say, how can such a flawed creature be one with its perfect Creator
Because, I say, because He deposited in us something of His greatness
Everything that makes me who I am leads me back to who He is
Life's basic rights, freedom, equality, justice
I write for the unheard and speak for the unspoken
I like to think that my words have the power to heal the broken
Like Jesus made the blind to see
Through the All-Eye Seeing human beings are made free
Free to be and discover His Essence deposited somewhere deep inside
Free to craft it and mold it to reflect His light
Free to bask

I Saw the Devil in my Room

I saw the devil in my room
In the form of a roach
I hit him with a broom
With a shoe and a remote

Yet the devil is immortal
Impossible to kill
I even tried spray
But we're at a standstill

He's a bebe kid
He don't die he multiplies
And he's probably in my bed
Creating little demon guys

I saw the devil in my room
In the form of a bug
I don't know what to do
Where's God with my hug?

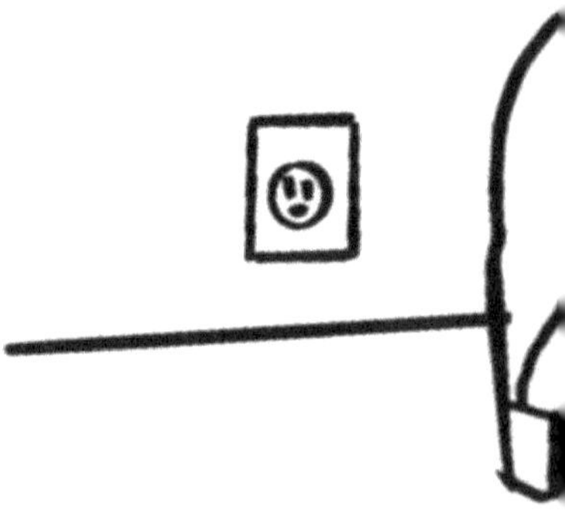

In a Room with God

Surrounded by four walls, boxed in, caved
With the only Being that can cause my grave
Death and life swirls around Him in a spiral
One hand holds the Qur'an, the other the Bible
Beneficent, Merciful, but also the number one Killer
The Destroyer, but also the Majestic Healer
Fear no one but Him I've been taught for years
And now when I face Him, I feel the fear
Because what if He judges me for my sins?
Prosecutes me because of the devil inside this Black skin?
Peaceful but yet wrathful, how can I understand
This Being formed from one single atom's hand?
That gave light but created Satan too
Just a lowly servant under His ultimate rule
But then He says, "As-Salaam Alaikum, peace,"
And so in a millisecond my fear is released

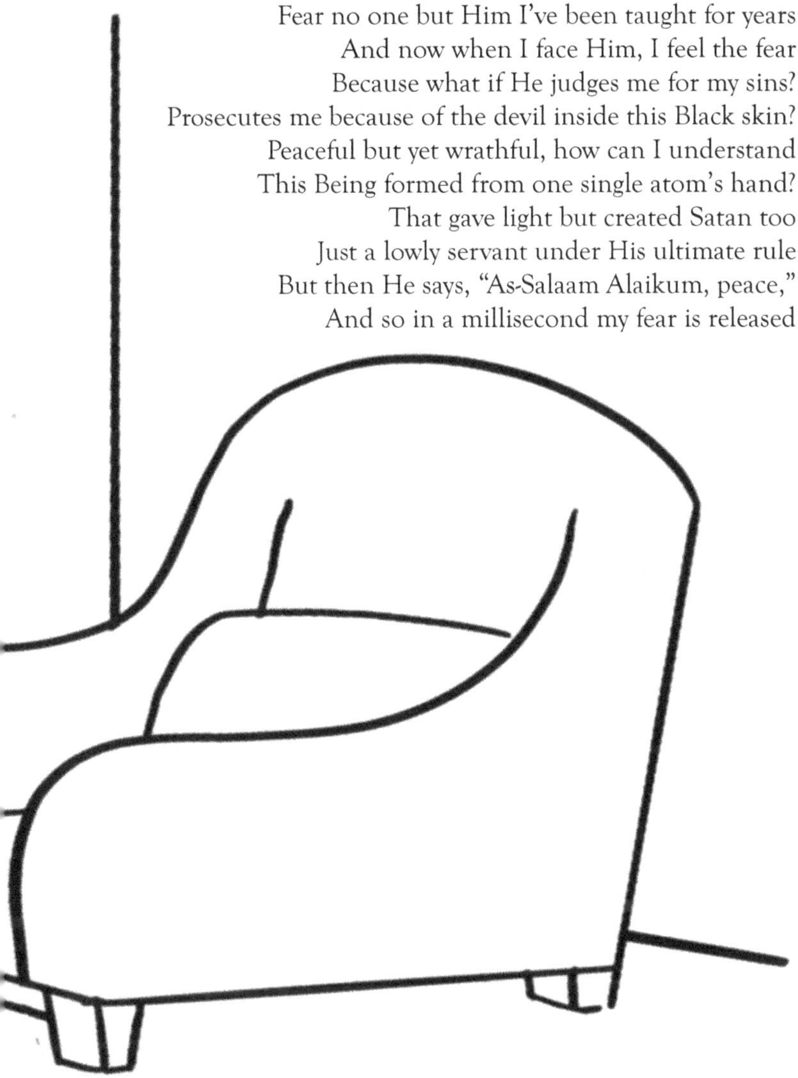

Let Us Create

They say when life gives you lemons, make lemonade
I say when life gives you a mustard seed, get down and pray
Get down on your knees and converse with God
Then plant that seed in good soil and sod
Bed it down and treat it right
Give it love and give it light
Then when it grows into a tree
Then, you'll see.

Tumultuously Chasing Perfection

Caught in the blades of life – spinning
Sweet air harshly caresses me – spinning
Vibrations blind and deaf me – spinning
Caught in the cycle of life – spinning
I'm turning, I'm flipping, where am I going?
I'm groggy, I'm bogged down, rowing and rowing
Swimming and swimming in the lake of fire
Chasing and chasing, balanced on the thin wire
I've reached it, I've reached it, reached what you ask?
Perfection – I bask.

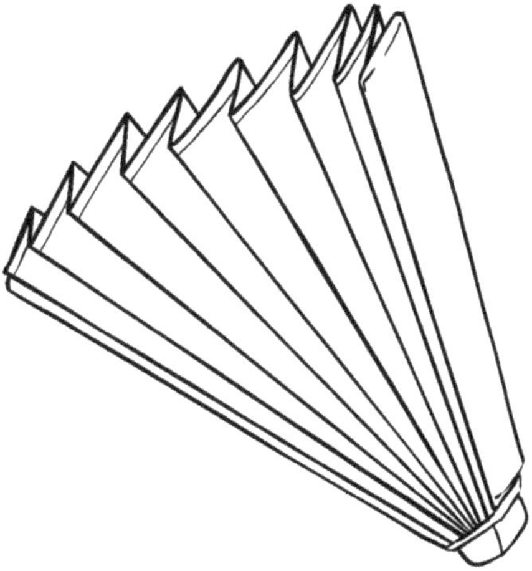

A Perfect Being

Blood makes a revolution in one minute
365 days makes an earth's orbit
Change, revolution, cells grow and die
Change, circulation, hellos and goodbyes
You're a new person every time a new thought is born
Some days you have roses and some days you have thorns
Be ye transformed by the renewal of your mind
Because real change starts when you and God align
Like the earth is pulled into the sun's orbit
You're suckled into God's grip
And He holds you tight and sends trials in your life
To strengthen, because change doesn't happen overnight
If blood makes a revolution in one minute
And if 365 days makes an earth's orbit
Then how long does it take Allah
To make the human being into a perfected god?

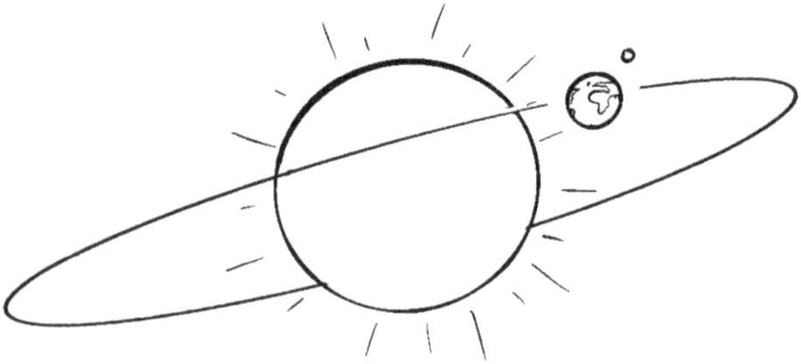

9. River

The War Between the Heart and Brain

Do you know the turmoil
Of a heart and brain
At odds against each other?

Neurons coil
And blood boils
At odds though they are brothers

Glial cells fight
Like hell
Against pale
White leukocytes

Do you know the grievance
Of a decision that has to be made
When the heart yearns for one thing
But the brain doesn't agree?

Follow your heart they say
Against the brain's plea
Follow your bleeding heart
While your neurons decay
Created in truth the brain cells
While your heart can follow lies
But follow your heart into hell
And let your glial cells cry

Do you know how hard it is
The time, the aches and pain it takes
To bring your heart and brain back again
Into one whole union?

A Bullet to the Heart

Decimation

Destruction

Devastation

Decline

Everything gone in between the finite time
Of a blink of an eye, or a bullet to the heart
The time between finish and start
The time it takes to pull apart
Two lovebirds singing a sappy song

But where is my happiness?
Why do I mourn
For a dead child not yet born
Because life didn't give him a chance?
Because I, didn't give him a chance?
I'm stuck in this trance
Dancing to death's dance
As I mourn
For a son
That was ripped and torn
From my cold bloody hands
If the midas touch turns everything to gold
Then what is the touch that decimates a soul?
That rips it from the body, that destroys
An unborn human boy?
I weep, I grieve away this pain so deep
That doesn't let the sun's rays wash away
A mother's fatal mistake

I was Eve, the doctor the snake
That whispered in my ear and caused such devastation

And what followed?

Hallucinations

As I dream of the unborn dead and the life he could have led

If I didn't let him be torn from my womb

Instead of a new world, this mother let him wake up to a dark, cold tomb

If the midas touch turns everything to gold
Then what is the touch that declines life to a soul
And the love birds sing their sappy song
Rock-a-bye baby
As they push the cradle
Down the cold dark street
I weep, I grieve away this pain so deep
A precious life taken between the finite time

Of a blink of an eye, the time between finish and start
The time it takes to pull apart
Two lovebirds singing a sappy song
The time it takes
To end this mother's life
With a bullet to the heart

Void

I cannot resist the pull of the black hole
Is it gravity or emptiness, I don't really know
Is it destiny or fate, perhaps a slave to fixed dates
Pulling me into the cyclical emptiness of hell's gate
A cycle I cannot escape
The menacing circle of blackness sucks life
Multiplies light into triple layers of darkness
Harken unto the demon
The formless void with Scorpion's arrow yelling get over here and keeping me from being a freeman
Huge masses of energy circle around me and yet I cannot tap into my own divine source of strength
Powers of 10, no 10 inversed unto itself until I'm in the negative tenths, thousands, millions
How could I have the galaxy at my foot yet paradoxically staring into this villainous void?
If wavelengths of light cannot avoid then what hope does a mere human droid have?
How could emptiness yet energy circle around existing in peace?
It's neither destiny nor fate for black holes exist beyond fixed dates
Perhaps it's my own grave mistakes holding me down like a weight
A demon that feeds on demonic energy while the divinity is bleeding from blatant wounds emptying itself of divine kinetics
That explains why I'm in cyclical motion but not moving
Being pulled yet stagnant in direction
Suffering from Black Hole Syndrome, an infection that plagues sanity
As the darkness rotates erasing my humanity
And leaving nothing but a droid
In a dark, cold void

Darkness

Darkness
But even in gross darkness energy surges
Even in gross darkness life emerges

Darkness
An atom was sparked in its divine womb
A seed under earth, then it blooms

Darkness
Cause adversity accompanies everything of value
Light shows what's hidden in the shadows

Darkness
That ignorant mind that needs to be shed
Be ye not conformed, renew the head

Darkness
What's done in the dark comes to the light
There's a reason why day precedes the night

Darkness
Secrets in the shadows are exposed
Day of Judgment, you reap what you've sown

Darkness
The peoples of the earth you keep perpetual slaves
But, remember when you were once in the caves

Darkness
No knowledge of self, living a beast life
Hidden history cuts like a knife

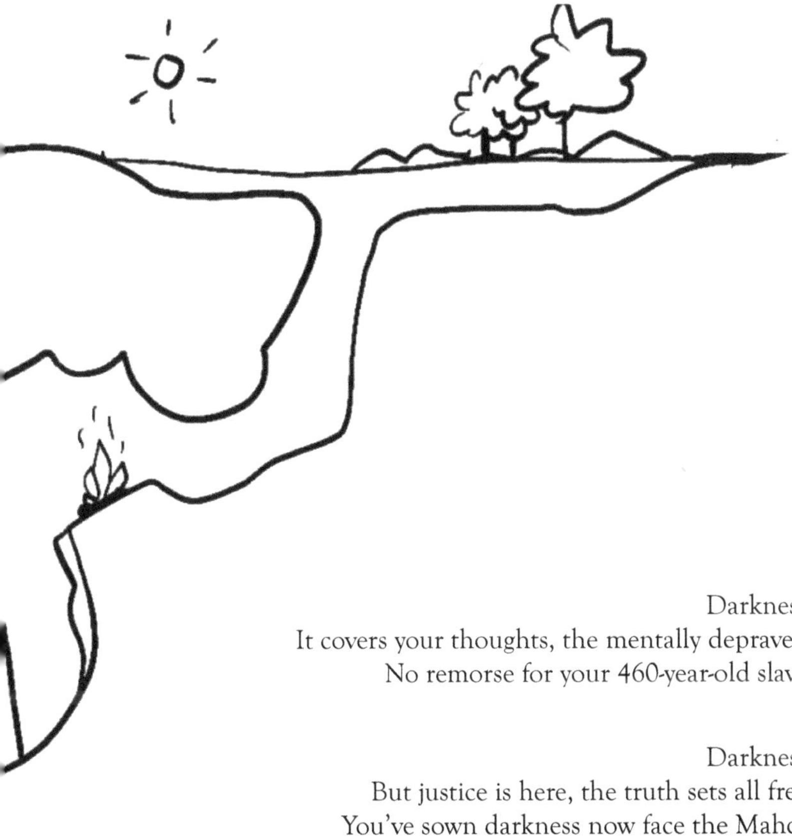

Darkness
It covers your thoughts, the mentally depraved
No remorse for your 460-year-old slave

Darkness
But justice is here, the truth sets all free
You've sown darkness now face the Mahdi

A Saviour was Born

Mahdi, Messiah, anointed to crush the wicked
400 years a slave, much pain was inflicted
Mahdi of the Muslims, the Messiah of the Christians
In 1877 a Saviour was born with a mission
Master Fard Muhammad was his name
Freeing the Black man and woman was his aim
God in the flesh came to save his people
God in the flesh came so we could exercise our freedom
Our servitude under the White man has ended
God in the flesh came so we could comprehend that
He made himself known at America's pinnacle
July 4th , 1930, to deliver the Original
Man back to his rightful state as God
He came in the person of Master Fard
Master Fard Muhammad manifested himself
Into Elijah Muhammad, who guided us into ourselves
Elijah Muhammad manifested himself into
Louis Farrakhan who is opening the eyes of the blind
He is redefining our frame of mind
This work started with one God, now we're a nation
With God's help we're moving toward our own salvation
Praise be to Allah for coming in the person
Of Master Fard with a determined purpose
We were 400 years a slave, much pain was inflicted
But a Saviour was born with the power to crush the wicked

It's Saviours' Day

Saviours' Day
Because I'm a saviour in my own way
Teaching, Guiding, New Wisdom is at play
On this day
That Master Fard was born
With a Mission to save the forlorn
The scorned
The worked and worn

Yes, it's Saviours' Day
Because you're a saviour in your own way
Elevating, Inspiring, Supreme Wisdom at play
On this day
That Master Fard Muhammad was birthed
To lift the burden from the earth
Create heavenly homes and hearth
Make all things new
Through
War, revolution
To perfect the human being's evolution
War, strife
Struggle is ordained for new life

Oh, it's Saviours' Day
Because a people cried, prayed
For the oppression to go away
The cry, the prayer
Birthed into the world a God that cares
About the condition, pitiful condition
So He came with a Mission
To set down every tyrant
Heaven on earth seems distant
But it's in the distance
Not far off
Closer
Everyday
Because it's Saviours' Day
And we're saviours in our own way

Praying to this Day

Black people prayed
For a Saviours' Day
A day of release from oppression
A day of receiving a blessing
Out of the womb of pain
A seed came
One born the God
Master Fard
Another born Elijah
The Exalted Christ and Messiah
Then Farrakhan came
To rain on the wicked's parade
Yes Black people prayed
For a Saviours' Day
A day to breathe from the chains
Someone to relieve them of pain
The coming of Christ
In men that's thrice
Prayed a prayer
God heard the tears and cared
So He came Himself to answer
Yes, Black people prayed
For a Saviours' Day
For Freedom, Justice, and Equality
Yes, Black people prayed
For a Saviours' Day
For release from their poverty
And the slaves, they prayed
For a Saviours' Day
A day their descendants would be free
And the prophets, they prayed
For a Saviours' Day
A day Satan would be crushed, hurray
And Black people prayed
And Black people prayed
And Black people prayed
For a Saviours' Day
To find out that day was today

Freedom from Hellfire

Problems arise, people die
Trials arise, people cry
Those who on Allah rely
Freedom from hellfire

Deliver Your Soul

What is the origin of the solar system, the sun, moon, and stars?
What is the nature of man and who are
You? Who am I? Who are we?
How can we bring into existence what we will when we say "be?"
Who makes rain, hail, earthquakes, and snow?
Who has the knowledge to make you light up and glow?
Who determines the diameter of your mind
The circumference of your activity? Who do you find
Raising the dead to life and making the dumb to speak?
Who heard your distraught cry in the wilderness, who heard your shriek?
Who came to your rescue, you who were despised and rejected?
Who cleaned you up, you who were a child neglected?
Who gave you that suit and bow tie, that white garment?
Who unlocked in you something that was lying dormant??
Will you teach the masses The Time and What Must be Done?
Will you go out into the wilderness and shine the light of the son?
What are you doing, sitting there wallowing in knowledge?
Look, a dead man! And one whose life is on the edge
Of the cliff! Wander the earth and spread what you know.
Do you have the Truth? Well, spread it. Deliver your soul.

Defining Beauty

What is beauty if it is the shell of a corrupted soul?
What is beauty if it doesn't shine forth from within?
What is beauty if you have no purpose and positive goals?
What is beauty if you're caught up in a world of sin?

But beauty in a man is that transformative power
You may have reached the 2nd floor but there's still a tower
Come to prayer, come to success, get reacquainted with God
Because simply put? Beauty is Farrakhan.

The Standard

I ask myself, I'm wondering
What the world is coming to
I ask myself, I'm pondering
Why another death is on the news
I ask myself, I'm wondering
How Donald Trump is on the rise
I ask myself, I'm pondering
Why you're falling for Clinton's lies
I ask myself, I'm wondering
How you're blind to the last days
I ask myself, I'm pondering
How you're blind to America's ways
I ask myself, I'm wondering
How Blacks live in constant oppression
I ask myself, I'm pondering
How Blacks forgive the White man's aggression
I ask myself, I'm wondering
But then the questions disappear
I ask myself, I'm pondering
But then Farrakhan makes everything clear
I listen to him, I hear him
And I receive my answers
I hear him, I listen to him
Because his words are the standard

Divine Servant of God

We have a man among us who is a Divine Servant of God
Allah, who came in the person of Master Fard
We have a man among us who is the representative of the Messiah
He's a lover of truth who exposes all liars
This love, instilled in him at birth
Pointing out to Black people our divine worth
Making sacrifices and putting the needs of the people first
Giving us the knowledge of self, God, and devil
Elevating the human being to the highest level
The level of God, coming into His thinking
Exposing the wicked in high places, exposing their stink
Bringing man to the brink of perfection
Closing the Gap between man and God, giving us the connection
Fulfilling prophecy and sealing up the books
The Time and What Must be Done exposing the true crooks
Leader of the young and the old, an example for the people
He sees through falsehood, his eyes are sharper than an eagle
Opening the eyes of the blind, making the deaf to hear
Sounding the trumpet, blowing so loud you can't mishear
Causing the dumb to speak and the lame to walk
Preparing us for the fall of this world, preparing us for the Shock
Of the Hour, leading an army, a nation
Building upon the foundation and working for the salvation
Of humanity, the greatest humanitarian you could find
Exposing the real anti-Semite and giving them a piece of his mind
In this day and time all eyes and ears should be on
This Divine Man, The Honorable Minister Louis Farrakhan

Empty Your Mind

They tell me to empty my mind
But how else will I find
The file that keeps me alive
That keeps my heart pumping
My blood jumping
From brain to spine
From spine to toe
The file that keeps me going?

Memories and moments
Feelings and longing
Deep-rooted sadness, sorrow
Unfulfilled happiness with the promise of a better tomorrow

Without the files of my brain
Tucked and stored away
In tiny little thought compartments
How else will I retain the memories and moments
That makes me, me

So even though we don't want the pain
And we want the happiness without the strain
We want to throw that sad moment away
And empty our minds as we walk around
As dead carcasses with no life and no sound
Waiting for a better day to be found
The memories and moments
Stored in your tiny little thought compartments
Are what makes you, you
So don't empty the mind
That keeps you alive
Don't throw away the file
That keeps your heart pumping
Your blood jumping
From brain to spine
Spine to toe
The file that keeps you going

I Live in the Now

Friends come and go
Relationships appear
Then disappear
Families grow apart
But one thing we'll always have are memories

Memories of the past
Memories of those gone friends
Memories of those disappeared relationships
Memories of family
But we shouldn't let our memories destroy us

Friends go but life moves on
I live in the now
Relationships break but life moves on
I live in the now
Families are tested but life moves on
I live in the now

I still laugh
I still cry
I still love
I still live

I look back at the past
I look forward to the future
But I live in the present
I am grateful for another day of living
I live in the now
Do you?

Believe Then Achieve

Don't forget about the past, but don't stay stuck
Look forward, and toward to what you can become
Don't let memories hold you back from achieving and succeeding.
Keep moving forward.
Everyone has difficulties in life,
But not everyone overcomes their difficulty
And becomes top of the world
But you can do it
If you just believe
Believe you can achieve
And you can fly
Spread your wings
Soar like the winner you are
You can do it
Just believe
Then achieve

By The Time

By the time, surely man is in loss except those who believe
Presently man has been deceived and its near impossible
For man's brain to conceive or perceive
That God is bringing about the destruction of this grievous
Country, this Mystery Babylon, modern day Rome

By the time, surely man is in loss except those who do good
Good has been mixed with evil and its near impossible
For the truth to not be misunderstood
We look at the world and don't know what we could or should
Do, in this Rome-like country, Mystery Babylon

Surely man is in loss, except those who enjoin one another
To Truth and patience, uncover
The blindfold from the mentally blind
Lift the veil from the confines of people's minds
Let the world see the beauty of Islam

Bismillah ir-Rahman ir-Rahim
By the time! – Surely man is in loss
Except those who believe and do good
And enjoin one another to Truth
And enjoin one another to patience.

10. SNOW

Purifying Seasons

Showers
Sun
Falling
Snow
The change of the purifying seasons

Winter

I feel like a conduit of dead energy
Though energy belongs to the living
Still, they disrupt my already disorganized entropy
And I become scattered
They are writhing, manipulating gray matter
Trying to infiltrate a living system
Yet my immunity is restricting
I can feel them trying to communicate with me
The dead rise out of winter's sea
It is known, it is felt
I can practically smell their snow-burnt flesh
The reeking scent of fresh blood
They have something they want to say
But how can transparent gas infiltrate black clay?
How can the sand's glass shatter through gray stone?
Yet it is felt, it is known
I can practically hear whispers on a dying breath
Neither alcohol, cigs or meth
Could copy what I sense
I can feel their touch breaking through my body's defenses
I can taste the snow in the air we share
I can see their eyes with beady stare
Prayers, praying, for what, for freedom?
A dom I don't yet have myself?
What can I offer you, snow-burnt beings?
To keep you from sucking my energy away?
To give you peace of mind from your own decay?
Rotting trunks, I see the dead as trees
Bumps and waves, they rise out of winter's sea
It is known, it is felt
I see the dead as they are
The night attracted to a living star

Night Sky

Night sky, glistening bright
It looks as if you are full of life
Night sky, oh how I love your light
Strike into people's souls like a knife
Night sky, up so high
Happy tears is what you make me cry
Moonlight, shining light from the sun
Last thing I see when my day is done
Oh, starry night, how beautiful you are
Good night, as I sleep under the stars

Night's Whispers

The night spoke to me in silent whispers
The dancing wind made me shiver
The singing crickets caressed me to sleep
I soon started seeing swaying sheep
Hoots from owls joined me in the world of dreams
Blissful world full of owls, crops, and lumpy cream

I Saw a Bee Knocking on my Bedroom Window

I saw a bee knocking on my bedroom window
As soft streaks of sun crept in
And mourning doves sung to the daylight's glow
As I lay in bed, energy spent
I didn't answer the bee's call to get up
Nor the dove's follow-up
I listened, lazy ear as the bee knocked once more
Yet I lay in my bed, lazy gaze to the floor
And after another bird's song to rise, to rise
I closed the blinds to my window then closed my eyes

Imagination

The darkness swept over me like a hawk does a mouse
The quiet mystified me
The unknowing darkness
My imagination as wild as could be
Lurking shadows turned into ghosts
Cars going down the street below
Transferred into monster roars
Dark corners where anything could hide
Tiny spiders that could crawl into my mouth
Everything reminded me of 'The BFG'
A book that wasn't scary at that time
Now scared me
Thoughts of the witch's hour at 12 a.m.
Thoughts of giants sticking their oversized fingers
Through my small glass window
Grabbing me
Pulling me
Eating me
But soon, I was asleep
Unaware of the imagination of my brain
Until the next night

Nectar in a Sieve

The unsung heroes in every woke Black poet's poem
They cry out from beyond the tombstone
A vampire's life is sweet compared to the dead beneath my feet
The vampire is dead yet alive, able to survive and thrive in the dead of night
He eats, he drinks, he kills, he lives
While the Black and dead are separated from life like nectar in a sieve
They're the unsung heroes in every woke Black poet's poem
As they cry out from beyond the tombstone
A zombie's life is saccharine compared to the dead beneath the shrine
The zombie is dead, yet alive, able to survive and thrive in the dead of night
He walks, he breathes, he eats, he lives
While the Black and dead are separated from life like nectar in a sieve
They're the unsung heroes in every woke Black poet's poem
As their woes bemoan the living beyond the tombstone
A ghost's life is rave compared to the dead in the grave
The ghost is dead, yet undead, haunting a life it already led
The ghost, he floats, he talks, he treads, he lives
While the Black and dead are separated from life like nectar in a sieve
Tell me why the monsters have a voice among the living
The mere ability to have the privilege of existing
Legs to walk and the ability to talk
In death they still have breath
Yet I can barely hold this thin piece of thread
Of what the Black and dead are saying and what they have said

And now I know the true bloodsucker is a systemic society built on
the backs of those that are deprived of freedom, justice and equality
The true zombie is a system built to deprive the oppressed of a brain
then rape them and take their culture and kill them and of course
they're the ones to blame
The true ghost is the lie that floats in and out of every Black person's
life that tells you about post-racial myths while your blood seeps
through society's invisible truths like sweet, sweet nectar in a sieve
Somehow the undead are still free to live, live, live, live
While my dead Black people are bled like nectars in a sieve forced to
cry a dying cry that can barely be heard beyond the tombstone
Forced to stay alive on the tiny threads of a woke Black poet's poem

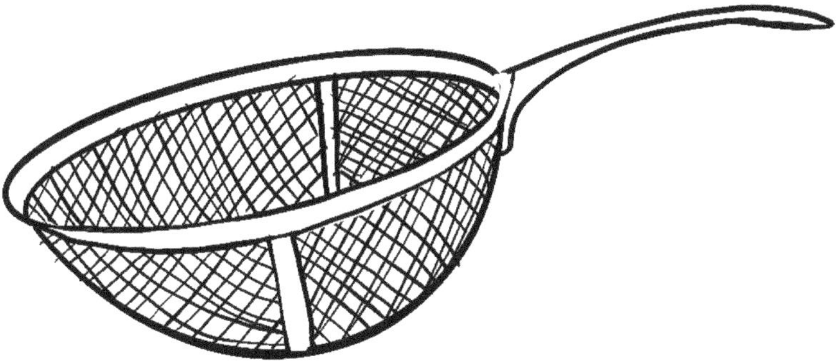

I Tried For Him

I cried for a man I never knew
I pain for the ones the devil slew
I tried for some but couldn't do
I tried for some but couldn't do

What kind of person am I
I, who am sensitive to Black death
Black bodies in the street, dark scenes with dying breath
Yet no tears are cried for my own uncle
Tragic, shot! Lies crumble
An already broken family heart
When Alton Sterling's family broke down, I broke down too
I shed more tears for a man I never knew
When my family broke down, I numbed my emotions
And when I felt, I upped the doses
Of the nonchalant medicine drops
The murdered corpse relies on cops
While family and friends scream for justice
And I just watch
I watch silently the erosion of my family
The sweet sting of decay
As my grandmother's body is still fresh in the grave
At his death
What kind of person am I
Me, who shed tears for Nipsey Hussle
But can't seem to contract my eye muscle
Me, who marinates in misery all the day long
But can't seem to hear the last breath of a life song
From a slain uncle
They send me messages "May Allah be pleased with him"
But how can He be pleased with him who sank in spiritual darkness
His carcass and I lie at a spiritual distance
For he was mentally dead long before the gunshot stole his life
He surrounded himself with demons and they plunged the knife

What kind of person am I?
Nay, what kind of person was he that God placed a protective shell around my heart?
Yet still I ask
What kind of person am I that

I cried for a man I never knew
And I pained for the ones the devil slew
Yet I tried for him but couldn't do
I tried for him but couldn't do

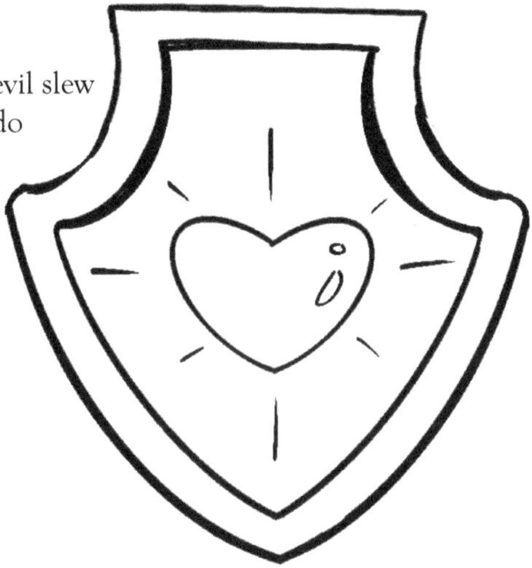

Open Season

Skin as brown as dust
They look at you
They judge you
Bang Bang
They shoot you down

Skin the color of dark chocolate
Stripped of name
Stripped of culture
Stripped of freedom
Stripped of justice

A child still yet to become an adult
Victimized and criminalized
Shot down by vigilantes
Shot down by law enforcement
Guilty by way of courts

Chained chocolate child
No protection from the law
No protection in the hood
A crime to walk in the night sky skin
Deaf, dumb, drained, and dead

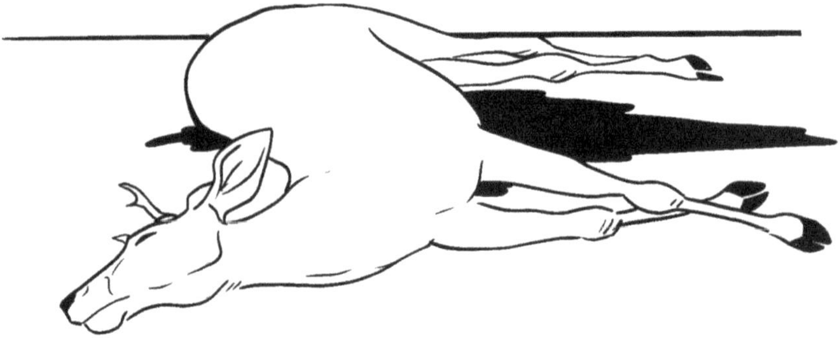

Sixth Sense

Little Black child
Do you hear your cry?
On the ground lying
A pool
Of blood

Little Black child
Do you see your bullet-ridden body?
On the street lying
A river
Of blood

Little Black child
Do you smell the stench?
Flesh
A sea
Of blood

Little Black child
Do you feel despair?
Dead
An ocean
Of blood

Little Black child
Do you taste metallic red?
Life
Evaporates
Into mist

Little Black child
Do you sense?
A last breath
Before
Freedom
—Return

Looking Death in the Face

His eyes are sunken
His countenance is fallen
A shell of the man he used to be

He's a restless soul
With sleepless nights
His dead son appears to him in dreams

There's never a day
That passes away
When he doesn't relive his child's murder

He walks with pain
He sees with pain
In the quietude, he mumbles to the slain

When you shoot a teen
An unarmed Black child
He's not the only one that dies

His family suffers
His people cry
Another leaf fallen from humanity's tree

You took a life
You're still free
Does the universe not feel my pain?

His eyes are sunken
As he lives zombie like
Reliving the day his son was slain

My Nightmare

I had a dream
It was misguided, but it was a dream
A dream that one day we could redeem race relations in America
So like Martin Luther King I slept and I dreamt but nightmares woke me up to reality
Like I don't understand why we're locked and we're chained when all we wanna do is be free
Yes, I had a dream, but the dream shifted to nightmarish pain
At the tender age of 14
When I saw a shot and killed Trayvon Martin on my TV screen

I watched the case closely, eyes like a lawyer as I cross-examined the prosecutor
The attorney, the witnesses and the shooter
I carried a tinge of hope in my heart, like no way, like maybe this one time
But Zimmerman got an acquittal so Trayvon's killer didn't do time
And the dream was shattered
Hope scattered on the wings of a black dove
Carrying all of our black tears to heaven above
I don't think you understand the pain of Black death on a Black girl's psyche
The way she hugs her brothers tightly
Because they could be next
Her older brother could be walking at night in his apartment complex
Holding a milkshake in his hand and somehow the moon transforms it into a gun
Then a White resident calls the cops and now he's done
A 14-year-old girl shouldn't have to hear the cries of a 17-year-old that died
She shouldn't have to watch his killer slide
As his mother screams and his family grieves
She shouldn't have to look into Mike Brown Senior's eyes and see something dead that can never be revived
When she looks at 12-year-old Tamir Rice she sees her 10-year-old brother playing in snowy ice
When a police officer does a drive-by shooting and deprives her brother of life
She doesn't understand why we're locked and we're chained, suffering from nightmarish pain when all we wanna do is be free
So like Martin Luther King she slept and she dreamt but nightmares woke her up to the reality
That little black boys and little black girls don't have the luxury of dreaming

Go to Bed Black Child

Little Black child, go to bed, the streets are crawling with clowns
Who want to use you, abuse you, they're all over town
Little Black boy, be safe from the civilized clown's courts
Legalizing evil of a different kind of sort
Black girl on the side of the road who needs help
Be weary of the clown-faced officer that beats the innocent into a pulp
Unrecognizable, your hair is wild and you have a red nose
Because the clown masqueraded as the law and partnered with the judge the scarecrow
Little Black children, go to bed, the streets are crawling with suffering and woe
Don't let your mothers become Bambi's Black doe
Dead at the hand of one with painted hair and painted face
Smiles on their lips as they get away with a murder case
Suspended with pay and found not guilty because murder is their employment
Creeping and crawling to find Black flesh because killing is their enjoyment

Dear Mama

Dear mama

I know you tried to raise me right
But they got me that night
Under lock and key
For a crime that I didn't see
Didn't hear
Didn't do

But dear mama
I love you

They manipulated you
To tell me to tell a truth
That I didn't hear, didn't see
You was tryna protect me
So I admitted
That I dropped to my knees and did it
And even though I didn't

Dear mama
I love you

I ain't had no food
No sleep, no you
A coerced testimony
Got me in a cursed matrimony
Between me and death
Can't catch a breath
The tears in your eyes
As I slowly die
In this jail cell
But dear mama
It wasn't you that failed

This country put a blade to my neck
When I was just a fleck, a spot
Just a mother's thought
And when I was born
The world gave you a warning
"Beware, animal"
And they passed that national
I was convicted
Before a guilty verdict was ever given
So dear mama

Dear mama
I love you

Dear Majesty

How would you feel
If your son was killed
Your heart sealed
Your pain like an onion peel
Your life a movie reel
But it's real

Your Black Magic being sucked away down an endless drain
Your pain slicing away at the edges of the seams of your mental brain
Sane
Sane
Sanity
Sanity – Sanity? – Sanity turned
Insanity
Humanity turned
Inhumanity
Dear Majesty, Dear Majesty
Dear White Supremacist Majesty

You dare make a travesty of my tragedy, making mockery
I loathe your
Joviality, your legal criminality dear White Supremacist Majesty
My son is dead, my son is dead yet you make mockery, vanity
You vain conceited –
This is not fantasy, this is my life, this is reality

My Black Reality

And yet there you sit
Cordiality
Where is the humanity?
How can I remain tactfully sane in my insanity as I weep
For my dead son

Weep
Weep
Weak
Sleep

Rock-a-bye Black boy, drinking iced tea
When the cop shoots, you will hang from a tree
Justice is broken, the country will fall
And down comes your Majesty, bloody and all

Rock-a-bye Black boy
My Black boy
Rock-a-bye asleep
In your forever cave, your grave
Ohhh, I'm in pain

Can't you feel my pain Mr. White Supremacist Majesty?
Your Majesty?
I don't think you'll ever realize
The gravity
Of this pain, the saneness of my insanity
The reality

Until you feel
How it feels when your son is killed
Your heart sealed
Your pain like an onion peel
Your life a movie reel
Then you question, is it real
Or is it
Sane
Sane
Sanity

My Mixed-Up Matrix

Red pill or blue pill? Which will break me outta this matrix?
To fight or to stand still? How can I overcome Satan's tricks?
Blue sky, white clouds, smooth lines with chemtrails
Cloudy sky, gray clouds, Black folks in jail cells
Cornfields and cotton days, modern plantation slaves
Why can't I just be free as the ocean waves?
Karate, Mortal Kombat, Lieu Kang on Satan's fangs
Robbed me of my history then you wonder why I gangbang
Genocidal plots got me Sonya Blading on Quan Chi
Original man, Black god, Queen of the planet that's me
My ebony skin and afro got you swinging mad blows
Vaccinations in a lying nation but one day you'll reap what you sow

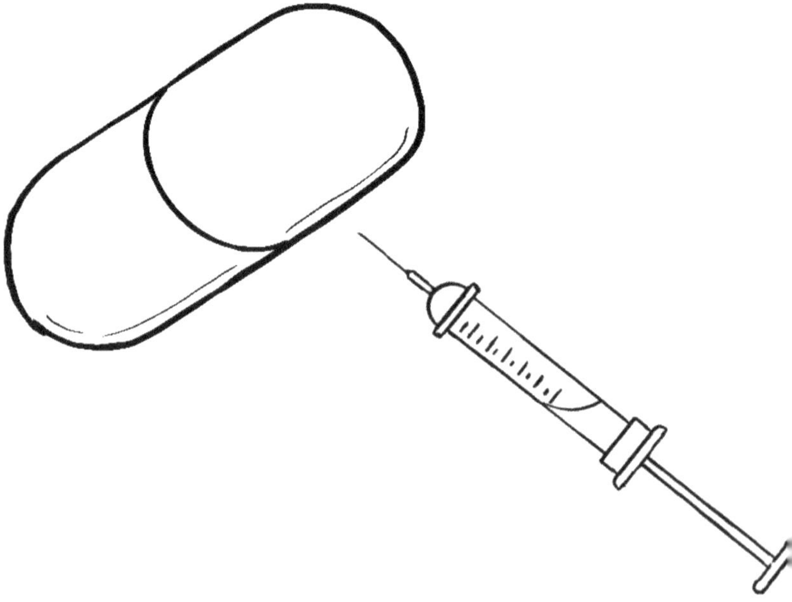

Ode Against Vaccinations

Vaccinations
Plaguing this nation with vaccinations
Gotta save this nation from vaccinations
Slaves to the pharmaceutical companies we are
America has a deep history of scars
From small pox against the native people of the land
Racist medical experiments on demand
Now we got flu shots targeting us
Just to put your little boy on a school bus
Mandatory vaccines causing sickness and disease
Mandatory vaccines giving companies cheese
While your little Black son develops autism
And the system ain't even working for him
Cause you on minimum wage with no health insurance paid
Just want him educated but you end up being played
Inject him with this and that until he has 32
Then you wonder why his immune system can't make do
Our babies are dying and we don't even have a clue
Not just Black but humanity at war against the few
Then you got government selling out their souls
Hillary Clinton calling for mandatory vaccines to role
You thought she, the wise hawk was on your side
But she smiles in your face while she secretly lies
The hawk that waits for the right moment to take the kill
To introduce mandatory vaccines in a bill
Can't even get an education cause of vaccinations
Demons plaguing this nation with cursed vaccinations
But what can you expect when a country's foundation
Is genocide, murder, and the Trans-Atlantic Slave Trade
Biological warfare and man-made diseases
Give you autism then cops tell you to freeze
Next thing you know you're dead and your mom says a prayer
Because they made you sick and the cop didn't care
From medical experimentation to HIV/AIDS
Children sick from disease while industries are paid
Vaccinations are plaguing this so-called great nation
Pharmaceutical companies make us all into slaves

Transformation

The rain creates a dismal atmosphere
Year after year it falls and smears
It transforms into snow, death in the cold
But then the day clears as a new world grows

11. CYCLONE

6-Day-Old Baby

Got a 6-day old baby ruling over me
The baby tells me to get down on my knees
I comply, I comply, but then he shoots me in the head
The 6-day old baby shot the Original Man dead

Got a 6-day old baby ruling over me
War and murder is all I see
Death follows the baby in all his bloodshed
The 6-day old baby shot the Indigenous man dead

Got a 6-day old baby ruling over me
Digging in the dirt and discovering the sea
New on the planet but a burden to the earth
The 6-day old baby is the opposite of birth

Got a 6-day old baby ruling over me
Destroying the land and poisoning the tree
New on the planet but a source of burden
The 6-day old baby is the world's worst vermin

Got a 6-day old baby about to reap what he has sown
Made a peaceful earth into a hostile warzone
He claims to be the oldest but he's actually a fraud
The 6-day old baby is about to meet God.

The Earth's Burden

Dead inside, dry and cracked
Water and flower cannot contact
Fire burns the petal away
Now it's time for the bees to pay

Dead inside, dry and cracked
The earth is having a panic attack
Fire burns the world away
Who told the devil it was time to play?

The earth's best-kept burden
Heaving and wheezing to spit out the vermin
In pain, in pain, crying in pain
Crying, crying, the tears, the rain
A nation in chains

In the womb of the earth
In the dead, dry, cracked womb of earth
A nation in chains
Water consumes, flowers bloom
And then its birth

Evicted

My life was doomed the day I was evicted from the womb
The powers that be sit in a dark room plotting my Black demise
The powers that see sit in a room seeing with black snake eyes
They write on their scrolls, dictating how to be racist
The White child is set up for success, the greatest of creation
The Black child gets when he's born chains and neck braces
We scream "I can't breathe" and they tighten the locks and throw away the key
Like the Dragon of Revelations, Dany's Mad Queen they tell us to "bend the knee"
Our education sets us up to trust the White Supremacist power structure
So we bend the knee to a school of thought that tells us that we're other
"You know nothing, Black Snow", you left your 'hood to another
They let you think you're corporate but you're still a Negro brother
White collar, blue collar, a black collar they use to strike down, veto
Your will, your independence, like the Walker and the Night King
Brainwash you into the system to keep you from flying on your wings
So little White boys can fall from trees and reach a raven's destiny
While little Black boys face police brutality and the officer gets "allegedly"

As soon as I was born they placed a mark on my arm labeling me for death
Savage, beasts, Dothraki lights went out in the night, that was their last breath
Ponytails and horses, I got woolen hair and Grand Theft Auto cars
I used to aim for lawyering but the teacher told me I couldn't be a star
A light went out in the universe, doomed the day my mama gave birth
How many children you tell that across this planet earth?
Just the Black ones? The Brown? Red, Yellow? Or White, too?
But we all started in kindergarten and only he took off and flew
Pride that Columbus sailed the ocean blue in 14 hundred 92
And killed the Natives of the land, but y'all don't tell that hidden truth
Then they learn their ancestors never told a single lie
Because White is pure and Black is bad so one can fly and one can die
But wait, Black can fly too, on the wings of a White savior dove
So the Breaker of Chains frees us then flies on her dragons high above
She frees us in one breath while murdering innocents with the dragon's breath
The physical chains are removed but how many dying from poisoned food?
Water, air, don't you hear the cry of the earth, don't you see the dark storms brood?
Rains, hurricanes, tornadoes and earthquakes, the birth pains pain
A nation evicted from the womb, a nation locked in chains

Eye of the Storm

I try to stay in the eye of the storm
Let it guide my form
As chaos reigns around me
Winds and rain uproot the tree
That stood tall 1000 years
But they can't reach my ears
Gossip tries to bite
And slander tries to strike
But the eye is my protection
Against diseased infection
That tries to get a hold
And has people catching colds
Of the ism-syndrome
They march to the tempo of Sexism
And they beat the drum of Racism
Getting wrapped in the cyclone's winds and rains
That uproots foundations and takes homes away
The eye is a shield against Classism and Ageism
Materialism, Ableism
Your mere human schisms do no affect me
In the eye, I am free, for I find serenity, peace
And I become blind to the chaos reigning in the streets
Blind but seeing as the All-Eye Seeing guides my steps
I listen when He talks and go where He goes, thoroughly trapped in His ebb and flow
Some prefer the eye of the tiger and the darkness of the night
But they don't know the eye of the storm, the quiet, the light
Of God, the true Champion of the fight
They don't know what it's like to see
Winds and rain uproot a tree
As chaos reigns around
Around but not through because God guides the form
As I stay
Secure
Watching
Waiting
In the eye
Of the storm

MATERIALISM
RACISM
CLASSISM
SEXISM
ABLEISM
AGEISM

Boat

Sharks circling,
Storm rampant,
But still chilling
On this rickety boat.

Titanic

She thought she was all that, she thought she was it
Until the people started to manic
In manic mania as the unsinkable sunk
Wooden pieces on the ocean blue, the ship's parts went plunk into the sea
Christopher Columbus reached beached shores in 14 hundred 92
And discovered a land people already knew existed
And somehow the thought originated that amidst nations falling like sinkable ships America is to be unsinkable
Like Noah's Biblical ark, forever invincible
But the thinker must not have known that all ships eventually return to the sea
That the sea even sets the land of countries free to breathe under its waves
With no hope of being saved

Footsteps

Fall of America, dollar on the decline
Fall of America, if only we would align
Combine
Our minds   With the Divine

Babylon the Great has fallen...has fallen
Help...help...she's falling and she can't get up
Falling and can't solve her problems
Fallen...fallen...with no help from above

Fall of America, systems corrupt
Fall of America, if only we would reconstruct
Abruptly disrupt
From the conduct   Of the unjust

Titanic...Titanic...the unsinkable has sunk
Help...help...she's sinking because of a hole
Sinking...sinking...in the water she goes plunk
Sinking...captain of the ship...has lost control

Fall of America, people insane
Fall of America, if only we would behave
Escape the decay
And restrain   From the afraid

Rome the superpower...has died
Help...help...but it's too late
Rome has fallen by the waist side
Was on life-support...didn't notice her state

Fall of America, she still has time
To get rid of the crime, the slime
Still a window
To align
Her mind   With the Divine

All She Wrote

He is Truth personified and you thought you could silence
You banned what? You thought you could try it
But Truth is a fire that burns wild and runs free
The Discrimination, no lock and no key
See you plan and Allah plans and Allah is the Best of Planners
See you plan and Allah plans, I wonder if you hear the clamor
They cry out, "Farrakhan," they cry His name in the streets
They cry out, "Farrakhan," do you hear the drumbeats?
The sound of your ship sinking into the great blue sea
Fires and floods, did you think you were the queen bee?
The unsinkable titanic lying on the ocean floor
She can't resurrect herself, the waters washed the oars ashore
Silencing the Truth won't help your boat stay afloat
You thought you could try it but that's all she wrote

He is Truth personified and you thought you could silence
You must've forgotten the majesty of the Lion
You must not know 'bout Him, you must not know
That He is the Beloved of God, that He got divine flow
The Sun that gives birth to the Stars in the Universe
He is not just one man but His light has dispersed
Into millions of people across this planet earth
I think I'm Farrakhan, so you might as well ban me, too
We are all Farrakhan, you can't put a cap on Truth
It's ok, it's ok, I hear you crying on your deathbed
Wow, look at that. I didn't know the devil bled
The unsinkable Titanic but there are holes in your boat
You thought you could try it but that's all she wrote

Call Me God

Call me Goddess without the dess
Dess, the outdated form of dais
Meaning a raised platform for the VIPS
But I'm not your princess, call me Queen
No, call me God, with Force and Power
It's time to come, no time to cower
Give birth to faith and murder fear
Devil dead in yesteryear
Leave the dess and call me God
The female form of Master Fard
Neelam said she'll be the king
I'm playing Chess, so call me Queen
No, dub me God and say ameen

God High

Flying, floating, I'm on that God High
Light as a feather, soaring through the sky
Elevating to elevated elation
That God High got me building a Nation
Farrakhan! Farrakhan! Now I see
Farrakhan! Farrakhan! Now I'm free

Flying, floating, I'm on that God High
Too busy looking heaven in the eye
What you know bout that, what you know?
Why you in the corner smoking that Satan Low?
I'm on that good kind of High, the God kind, the good stuff
But you on that 'hood kind of High, smoking the devil's puff
Satan, Devil, pick your poison, you're in hell either way
God, Allah, offers healing and the promise of a better day

Listen to Kendrick Lamar, the boss says be humble
Be humble, be humble, submit to Allah, cry uncle
So you, too, can fly, float, hover on that God High
So you, too, on god status, looking heaven in the eye

The Black Rose

Freedom; Fantasy
Red rose, bow to the black rose
Life enslaved to death

My Shadow

The dark soul moved as I moved
Stood still as I stood still
My hand reached out to touch it
My hand got lost in its darkness
I felt the breeze underneath the shady tree
I walked out
Out into the open
I looked for the dark spirit
Nowhere in sight
My hand reached out and touched emptiness
The light of the sun scared away the figure
It was now lost out there in the universe
My second self
My shadow

Disconnect

Footsteps
You disconnect yourself
Where do you go?
My second self, my shadow
I look out the window
A princess caged from suffering
But you walk through the people's woe
And you return with utterance
You see all, know all
Through the night's streets you crawl
Hiding in broad daylight
To understand my people's plight
I'm locked but you're free
I'm blind but you see
And even as I look out this window
I see the poor, the torn, the weary and worn
You are the fraction of me that will take action
Against my country's factions and the wicked plans that are hatching
Go my shadow, go, tell the king it's time for war
Go my shadow, go, tell the queen I've closed the door
Go my second self, my shadow
Disconnect yourself
Let me hear your footsteps
Let this princess rule her colony
Let me hear the footsteps of equality

War of Armageddon

Can you smell it in the air?
Through the whispers and despair?
It's on the horizon
But no one is realizing
The War of Armageddon
Is spreading
The White man is shedding
His façade, and now we see the naked truth
At war with Islam and Black youth
On the rocketship to hell
It's too late to ring the bell
Under God's spell
Of death, the rider of the pale horse
Taking us on an apocalyptic course
I can smell it in the air
Through the whispers and despair
Wars and rumors of war
Floods washing people ashore
Tornadoes soar
Hurricanes burst through your living room door
Rain floats the floor
The shock of the hour
Now we're under God's power
We failed to head the message
So we're facing America's wreckage
The War of Armageddon
Is spreading
The White man is shedding
The Black man is not separating
So God is generating
Rain, hail, snow, earthquakes
So God is generating
Aches and fiery serpents and snakes
The War of Armageddon
Is spreading
Just smell it in the air
Through the whispers and despair

Freedom, Justice and Equality.... Or Else

Give me Freedom, Justice and Equality or else it's war
Justice is God's weapon to tear up your root and core
You reap what you sow, sow the wind, reap the whirlwind
Submit to the law of Justice, can't beat the hurling
Of the Truth at your brains, knock that falsehood out
Until your remains are suffering from drought

Give me Freedom, Justice and Equality or else it's war
God will use Justice to rip your heart from your core
In the Last Days, men's hearts will fail them with fear
Because you've raped and robbed, now it's your time of year
You reap what you sow, get back 10 times what you sent
But, God is Merciful, there's a little time to repent

Give me Freedom, Justice and Equality or else it's war
My cry is Justice or else the flood will wash you ashore
The Trans-Atlantic Slave Trade was a crime against humanity
Then you put a White Jesus as the face of Christianity
You reap what you sow, you'll get back what you put out
Death is at your door, famine, pestilence and drought

Give me Freedom, Justice and Equality or else it's war
Or else the ark will pass you, you'll be left ashore
Or else God will send the forces of nature after you
Or else you will wish that your actions you could undo
Or else you will reap what you've sown on God's people
Or else death will pass to you as we gain our Freedom

You refuse to give us Justice, so it's time for war
Come against us and we'll rip your heart from your core
Law of Retaliation, fight with those who fight with us
If you put a knife to us, don't expect not to get cut
If you shoot us down, don't expect to live after that
No more Black lives shed without us fighting back
Can't win in a war against the Original, Black don't crack

Can't win in a war against God, you're up against His belt
I suggest that you give us what we humbly ask: Justice...or else

Young, Free, and Black

Young, free, and Black so they're on the attack
Got a system in place that keeps my people in the back
Midnight skin, now I'm assault rifle's snack
Pharaoh's after me because I'm young, free, and Black

Free, Black, and young so they suck the breath out my lungs
Don't have a voice, no sound, no tongue
The caged bird sings but I'm dead without a song
Pharaoh's after me because I'm free, Black, and young

Black, young, and free so they shoot me down in the street
I'm a god, I'm a god, that so? Then how come I'm beat
Dead at 12, 17, 22 before I'm entirely complete
Pharaoh's after me because I'm Black, young, and free

Young, free, and Black so they're on the attack
Free, Black, and young so they suck the breath out my lungs
Black, young, and free so they shoot me down in the street
Pharaoh's after me, so the "or else" I will be

Haiku Series on War

The sky is blood red
Preparing for the great war
The clouds are ready

Did you see that guy
A villain asking for more
He thrives on darkness

His puppets taunt us
Psych us out of the great war
Prepare, prepare now

But we have offense
To say we don't is folklore
Prepare, prepare now

The sky is blood red
Prepare for your destruction
The clouds are ready

Battle in the Sky

Chaos reigns in the streets
The drumbeats of war
Sound the song of the trumpet
The devils congregate in their tent
They make plans to come at you
From before you and behind you
From your right and your left
But you let them in, as your guests
You let demons consume the flesh of your brain
They make evil fair-seeming and cause you pain
Four devils lie in your heart
They tear the gods of self apart
Devouring all signs of divine energy
And you become lethargic
A vegetative state
And you stay that way until heaven's gate opens
Letting in light, the Son
And the war is won

11. SEA

Haiku Series on Freedom

1.
Words on the sweet breeze
In beginning was the Word
And then God said "Be"

2.
Time–sting like a bee
To get some equality
Be strong like the tree

3.
Freedom, let me see
Black Power is the real key
Time for unity

4.
God said "Be," it is
Still we rise is what will be
Kings and Queens we are

5.
Birth forth stars that shine
We walk the line of divine
Complete above said

Standard Operating Procedure

How can I be a complete being when I identify as a robot
Formed from mechanic bits and parts
I block my feelings to protect my heart
But sometimes the tears try to break through the wall
Sometimes it cracks and the bawls peek through
Shattered glass blew
And left a mass of withering metal behind
And this mechanic being is left to pick up its broken design
Its broken bits and pieces blown by wind
Left to its own devices to mend its own brokeness
And to try to rebuild from the extreme distress of its own mess of emotions
And it fixes and reconstructs and rebuilds until it's once again in motion
And its ocean once again hides behind thinly constructed walls around the heart
Because robots are fragile creatures
And one cracked dam could break its standard operating procedure apart

Stained

A raindrop dripped
And shielded my tear
Water merged with salty water
And inside its figure
Shimmered past, present, future
I saw love gained and love lost
Love tamed and love tossed
Love's expansion on a rooftop mansion
Love's compression and its digression
I saw familial love and romantic love
Affectionate love and misdirected love
True, false, humble, boastful
Poison, real, all and total
Every form of love imagined
Every tear and every laughter
Love hurting and love healing
All of this the drop revealing
Shimmering past, present, future
Inside its hourglass figure
Water merged with salty water
Shielding my tear; dripping, dripped
And water left its tear-stained whisper
Like rain shimmering in a mirror's eye
Dripping on my crying soul
Dripped; dripping, whilst all behold

The Mask

She wears the mask made of silver with ebony eyes
She wears the mask to shield herself from friends and enemies alike
She wears the mask to disguise the truth within
What lies beneath the depth of midnight skin
Under the mask she is a different being
Stiff, robotic, she thinks she's free but she's unseeing
The mask is an umbrella that both protects and destroys
It is her camouflage, allowing her to pose as a metal decoy
To keep her emotions under control
Her soul is trapped and tinged with steel
She can't cry, can't bleed, repressed emotion, no feels
And it keeps people away from her but it also keeps the real
They pretend they don't see the mask, they look past its silver and black
And they learn her in stages, but still they know she's holding back
Close yet far away, she holds them hostage at an emotional distance
But the real push through like the resistance sent to embrace her existence
Because how dare she waste away in metal cast
And waste away behind the mask

Traveling

My meanness is a mask for the glass menagerie hidden inside
Evil thoughts transfer to evil words on the tongue
For a moment I speak a strange language leaving the other person stung
A protection and defense to shield the weakness of myself
I channel a façade of strength taken from the characters that linger on my bookshelf
Conceal, don't feel, don't reveal your inner truth
Make sure they know you have no soul, you're nail and tooth
You can survive off of fake smiles and fake laughs
It's better than opening yourself up to pain then getting stabbed
Between a choice of love and hate just go with hate
Because love can leave us trapped in a cage with no escape
Our shields scare friends and foes alike
But true friends look past the mask to see the glass menagerie hidden inside
My protection to keep the menagerie upright
Their strength travels across a line of wires to give me fight
Like a character at the end of a story I'm able to shine my inner light
And I escape Caged-Bird-Syndrome and take flight
Rising
And rising
And risen—to a great height

7 Rings

There are times when I feel dark, down, depressed and despair
But like a rose's thorns my sisters wrap around me, shielding me in a protective cocoon
And serve as the oxygen to my air
We go through our honeymoon phase of laughter and sweet bliss
But even when we frazzle each other's nerves and feelings get hit we are still seven rings
Seven rings, seven crowns, seven queens sitting on thrones
Our DNA is made of gold

Dark, down and depressed but they lift me up out of my drowning sea of repressed emotion
Unknowingly they help me ride the waves of my self-created ocean
And I come out on land dry
Seven branches point up to the sky and travel down through the earth until there is a single root
Fruit of the same tree, rings, wings, jewels given by God to fly into our own heavenly existence
A place in the distance where darkness and depression is forbidden
Where the rings reflect the Son's light and the wings take to the skies
Where everything gold can stay and nothing gray can stay alive
And seven rings, seven crowns, seven queens sitting on thrones are able to thrive

The Majestic Oak

Nature's peace, her serenity
Shine light on my self-identity
Illuminates my self-divinity
As I look to the majestic tree
Tall with firm oak, a ladder to the heavens
Its leaves a trampoline to God's humble den
To knock on the door, to be let in
To dote on the majestic oak tree within
At war with the willow who wears a weeping cry
I'm over sorrow, these days I fly high
Soar through the skies on the bark of the oak tree
To see the God within, to be truly free

Ode to Freedom

Wind in my hair
The vast sky above
The running mare
The heart-shaped dove

Smile on my face
Looking at the clouds
The squirrels race
The mama bird is proud

Dancing in the grass
Shouting, "I'm free!"
I broke the glass
To escape to the sea

Future's Promise

Sailing my way to future's promise
Paying homage like Future's I'm just being honest
The waves pick up and now I'm a comet
On fire, on fire, finding solace as sonic
And then the boat docks, I've arrived
In future's promise I thrive

The Red Sea

As the storm surges and upsets the Sea
Its electric charge diverges the waters and uproots a tree
The path becomes clear, and I stroll down
A golden sphere appears, with a golden crown
The sphere serves as a protective bubble
The crown, a queen's struggle
As she walks to reclaim her own

As the earth groans and stones are thrown
I walk, head high, to reclaim my throne
Through trials, tribulations, the electric Red Sea
When the waters diverge, I become free
Because the Lord's protective bubble surrounds my being
Causing me to see well beyond my eyes
As I walk to reclaim my throne

As the earth groans and the storm winds blow
I walk, head high, to reclaim my own
The winds burn my beating heart
And the fires freeze my world apart
Yet onward I march through the diverged Red Sea
Through the Middle Passage, seeking to be free
As I walk, I march, to reclaim my throne

As the storm surges and the Sea divorces
I walk, head high, down the chartered course
Through chains, slavery, lynches and Jim Crow
Through trials, tribulations, the Sea's ebb and flow
The path becomes clear, as I stroll down
I've conquered the Middle Passage, I have my crown
And I've reclaimed my own

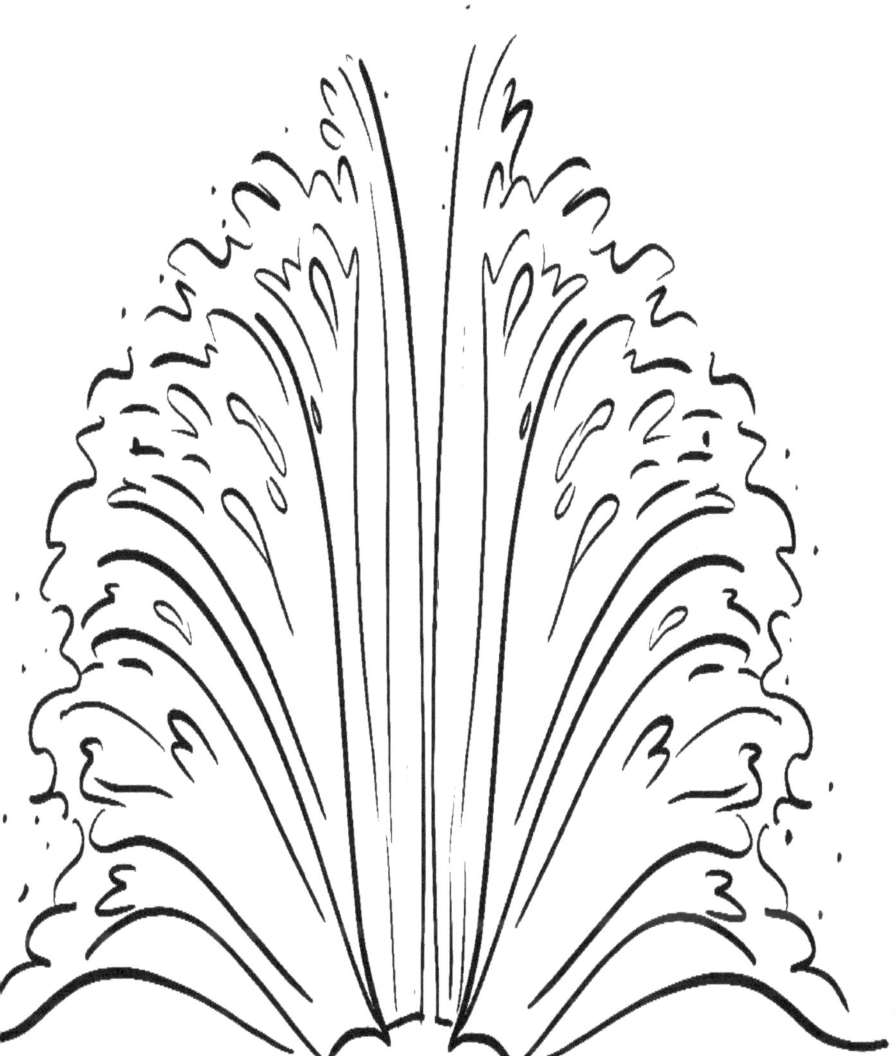

About The Poet

The umbilical cord wrapped around her neck at birth
Yet she did not surrender to the chokehold of death
She has gone through many trials and triumphs
An all-around writer: journalist, poet, author
With ease she alters words on a page and does her peers a favor by serving as grammar police
She loves to write about God and express her Islam which is peace
She can be found joking around with her five siblings
She spent her rare free times in college watching Netflix or a Marvel movie
She loves anything with a good story; especially when she's the one who wrote it
She is good with words although not so good at speaking
She took speech lessons in kindergarten to conform to society's views of properly conducted sounds
And she believes that maybe if the cord had not wrapped around
The she that is me
Wonders maybe
Maybe I would be less inclined to hide myself under a blanket of poetry
I could talk as free as the bird sings and never experience the self-diagnosed history of social anxiety
I could breathe fresh air then let the world carry the harmony of a sweet word spoken
I could go here and there singing the song of my voice
But see, the problem
The problem is
If it had not coiled around my neck like a boa constrictor squeezing its prey
If speech lessons and anxiety were erased
Would I still value the words I write and the spoken ones I say?
See, the problem
The problem with wondering 'maybe' is
If that other future happened
Would I still be... me?

Acknowledgments

Welcome, dear reader. You've made it to the end, whether you got here by reading each and every poem, by skimming or by immediately turning to this page. Either way, I thank you for picking up this book.

This book has been a labor of love. They say parents shouldn't have favorites, but as an author with many babies, now, I think that this one may very well be my favorite. I've been told so many times really since my teenage years that I should write a book of poems. And I've put one together several times. Even went so far as to name them.

But they weren't fulfilling what I envisioned. The full vision was, "I'm not releasing a peotry book until I can have an audio version to accompany it and illustrations for the poems." And I almost gave up on that vision with Troubled Waters. I want to thank my blood sister, Aliyyah, who encouraged me to enact my full vision of including drawings. I initially tried to illustrate it myself, despite the fact that I'm bad at drawing. I thank my friend Khadijah Muhammad for recognizing my bad artwork and for recommending Holiday Muhammad. I want to thank Holiday Muhammad for working with me in illustrating this book. I personally believe she is an artistic genius. I thank all of those who donated to help me raise the funds to pay her.

I thank Angela 8X from Washington, D.C. for reviewing both versions of the book (written and audio) and providing her feedback.

I thank the Seven Rings for helping me to come up with the title for this book, giving me feedback on the cover, supporting my journey and always hyping me up in my endeavors.

I thank everyone who has shown support throughout the time I spent working on this book.

Last and most, I thank Allah who came in the person of Master Fard Muhammad, the Christ and Messiah the Honorable Elijah Muhammad and the Jesus in our midst today the Honorable Minister Louis Farrakhan.

Thank you!!!

The Poet's Other Babies

- Escaping the Chains
- Chasing God
- Jewels to Jannah: Storybook
- How to Give Birth to an eBook in 9 Easy Steps

Visit amazon.com/author/anisahmuhammad to purchase!

CPSIA information can be obtained
at www.ICGtesting.com
Printed in the USA
BVHW062244050721
611175BV00021B/415

9 781737 353409